the
cooperative

SPORTS
&
GAMES

book

OTHER BOOKS BY TERRY ORLICK

The Second Cooperative Sports & Games Book
Every Kid Can Win (with Cal Botterill)
Winning Through Cooperation
In Pursuit of Excellence

the
cooperative

SPORTS
&
GAMES
book

Challenge Without Competition

Terry Orlick

PANTHEON BOOKS / NEW YORK

Library of Congress Cataloging in Publication Data

Orlick, Terry.
The Cooperative Sports and Games Book.

Bibliography: p. 121
Includes index.
1. Games. 2. Family recreation. I. Title.
GV1201.07 793 77–88771
ISBN 0–394–42215–5
ISBN 0–394–73494–7 pbk.

acknowledgments

So many people have been involved with our cooperative-games movement that it is difficult to know who contributed what, or how to give much-deserved credit. It has truly been a cooperative effort. At our Ottawa base we have created games, modified games, and extracted games from others. I am deeply indebted to all those who have worked with me in the quest to humanize contemporary games. Though they are too numerous to mention by name, they hold a special place in my heart.

In some cases we have extracted games from sources outside our immediate experience and were able to track down the sources. I would like to acknowledge gratefully these sources: Ken Burridge for Taketak; Jack Coberly for Parachute and Shake the Snake; Dan Davis for Cooperative Balance-Beam Activities; Jim Deacove for Cherry Bowl, Deacove Rounders, and Pin; Andrew Fluegelman and the New Games Foundation for Human Knots, Aura, Ecoball, Hug Tag, and Water-Balloon Toss; Gerry Glassford for Eskimo Games; Marta Harrison and the

Non Violence and Children Program for Gesture Name Game, Pru-ee (Tweetie), Nonverbal Birthday Line-up, Human Pretzel, and Water-Cup Pass; A. A. Mac-Farlan for Choosing Sides; Pierre Provost for Human Supports and Long, Long, Long Jump; Ian Robertson and L. Ager for Aboriginal Infinity Marbles; and A. Rosensteil for New Guinea Games.

I would like to extend special thanks to those who have been most instrumental in the creation, testing, refining, and distribution of our cooperative games: Cathi Foley, Sally Olsen, Jane McNally, Roberta Haley, Pierre Provost, Joy Slack, Marc Blais, Barb Lavergne, Kim Stairs, Penny Kome, and Barb Champion, as well as the Bayshore Nursery School, participating schools of the Carleton school system, and Wendy Wolf of Pantheon Books. There have been as many cooperative people as cooperative games, which is why we have been able to move ahead.

contents

ix

the
cooperative

SPORTS
&
GAMES

---

book

who needs games
nobody loses?

Have you ever seen the fun torn from a child's game? Have you ever seen children left out or put out by games, rejected, intentionally hurt, and wondered why? Then the games in this book are for you! They have grown out of these concerns and provide a positive alternative to competitive games. What's so different about these games? They are games of acceptance, cooperation, and sharing that can bring children, families, and communities together in the spirit of cooperative play. They have been carefully created, selected, and refined so that children can have fun while learning positive things about themselves, about others, and about how they should behave in the world.

The main difference is that in cooperative games everybody cooperates . . . everybody wins . . . and nobody loses. Children play with one another rather than against one another. These games eliminate the fear of failure and the feeling of failure. They also reaffirm a child's confidence in himself or herself as an acceptable and worthy person. In most games (new or old) this reaffirmation is left to chance or awarded to just one winner. In cooperative games it is designed into the games themselves.

My concern throughout this book is as much with the quality of children's lives as with the quality of children's games. Games can provide beautiful occasions for challenge, stimulation, self-validation, success, and sheer fun. This is what cooperative games are all about.

Although games have been played cooperatively in many cultures for centuries, there are very few games being played in our culture today that are designed specifically so that all players strive toward one common, mutually desirable goal. Genuine cooperative games with no losers are extremely rare in the Western world. Their rediscovery is something we can look forward to and gain from.

The first cooperatively structured games that I encountered were ones I played with the Inuit (Eskimo) in remote regions of the Canadian Arctic, and ones I created myself. The cooperative games created for this book came primarily from my work (and play) with students, parents, teachers, and children from different parts of the world, over the past five or ten years.

The beauty of these games lies in part in their versatility and adaptability. For the most part, cooperative games require little or no equipment and virtually no outlay of cash. They can be used with a wide range of populations and in a variety of physical settings. Anyone can play them, almost anywhere. The "rules," or nonrules, of the specific games need not be strictly adhered to. You can work out your own specific details. You don't need a certain kind of ball to play with or a definite kind of field to play on. You don't even need to play in pre-determined positions or for pre-set time periods. These things really don't matter. The important thing is the concept behind the games.

Patience may be needed to learn this "new" form of play, particularly if the participants have never before played cooperatively. However, with appropriate challenges, enlightened supervision, repeated exposure, and players' constructive input on cooperative changes, the games will begin to take off on a positive note. Once people make the transition and begin to play cooperatively, supervision and rule concerns usually become extremely minimal. The players begin to "supervise" and "officiate" their own behavior and also become concerned with one another's safety.

The games presented throughout this book have been designed and field-tested with children, but they are not restricted to children. Many teen-agers and adults may wish to revisit their childhood or enrich their adult lives through some of these fun-filled ventures.

The age categories outlined for the games should serve as only a rough guide. Specific game selections or adaptations can easily be made by children, adolescents, and adults of all ages to ensure that the games are (and continue to be) appropriately suited to the specific needs of the group.

The Need for Alternatives

As the factory has come to be a model for the organization of so much of Western life, so too have children's games been industrialized. The emphasis on production, machine orientation, and overspecialization has become as widespread in games as in industry. Games themselves have become rigid, judgmental, highly organized, and excessively goal-oriented. There is no freedom from the pressure of evaluation and the psychological distress of disapproval. In the end, the focus on squeezing the most out of every individual leaves no room for plain old fun.

Pitting children against one another in games where they frantically compete for what only a few can have guarantees failure and rejection for the many. Many children's games and programs are in fact designed for elimination. Many ensure that one wins and everyone else loses, leaving sport "rejects" and "dropouts" to form the vast majority of our North American population. To make things worse, the games are now beginning to destroy even the winners. Children are encouraged to delight in others' failures. They hope for it, they help it happen, because it enhances their own chances of victory. Exposing young children to irrational competition does not teach them how to compete in a healthy manner; it merely pressures them into competition. As they grow older, they have been so conditioned to the importance of winning that they can no longer play for fun, for enjoyment. They don't know how to help one another, to be sensitive to another's feelings, or to compete in a friendly, fun-filled way, even when they want to. If failure ensues, and it often does, many children learn to avoid competition, to withdraw. Failure at games may also "teach" children totally unjustified "bad things" about themselves.

Children nurtured on cooperation, acceptance, and success have a much greater chance of developing strong self-concepts, just as children nurtured on balanced diets have a greater chance of developing strong and healthy bodies. Should we really give young children unhealthy or unbalanced diets at the start ("so they'll get used to it")? Or let them develop in as healthy a manner as possible, for as long as possible (before they are conditioned to junk food)? When bodies and minds are still in the process of being formed and developed, isn't it better to give every child a firm base from which to start? Won't this enable him or her to meet and cope better with a variety of situations later in life?

In a study of successful and unsuccessful high school football candidates, Harvey Scott from the University of Alberta concluded that

> the unsuccessful sporting experience seemed to result in a strong spread of negative effect to other aspects of the self. For the majority of the boys who tried out with the teams and who of necessity failed, the tryout was a self-destructive rather than a self-enhancing experience.... The character-building effects of the successful in sports often seem to be gained at the expense of the cuts and dropouts, who must somehow build these failures into their self-systems.

In still another study, Howie Hyland at the University of Ottawa found that 8th-grade children who opted out of physical education had lower self-esteem, lower perceptions of sports ability, and more negative perceptions about their bodies than their peers who elected to take physical education. It is likely that these negative self-perceptions were influenced at least in part by exposures to failure or rejection in play and games, as children spend so much time playing in their developmental years.

The findings of studies such as these emphasize the need to develop individual games and whole sports programs in which all participants can be accepted and experience at least a moderate degree of success. If children think they have won, there is no need for them to feel threatened or anxious, and every reason to feel happy with themselves and satisfied with the experience. The fear of failure, along with the distress and frustration associated with failure, is reduced when errors are not viewed as a life-and-death matter. Cooperative ventures where there are no losers, along with friendly, low-key competition, which reduces the importance of outcome, frees children to enjoy the experience of playing itself. They are given a new freedom to learn from their mistakes rather than to try to hide them. When children know that their value as a person will not be shattered by a game score, games and playmates can be approached in a new light.

There are four essential components to a successful cooperative game: cooperation, acceptance, involvement, and fun.

WHY COOPERATION?

Cooperation is directly related to communication, cohesiveness, trust, and the development of positive social-interaction skills. Through cooperative ventures, children learn to share, to empathize with others, to be concerned with others' feelings, and to work to get along better. The players in the game must help one another by working together as a unit—each player being a necessary part of that unit, with a contribution to make—and leaving no one out of the action to sit around waiting for a chance to play. The fact that children work together toward a common end, rather than against one another, immediately turns destructive responses into helpful ones: players feel that they are an accepted part of the game, and thus feel totally involved. The result is a sense of gaining, not losing.

WHY ACCEPTANCE?

Feelings of acceptance are directly related to heightened self-esteem and overall happiness—just as rejection is directly related to a decline in self-esteem. In cooperative games, each child has a meaningful role to play within the game, once he or she chooses to become involved. Each child is also at least partially responsible for the accomplishment of a goal or successful outcome of the game.

WHY INVOLVEMENT?

Involvement is directly related to a feeling of belonging, a sense of contribution, and satisfaction with the activity. Being left out, eliminated, or ignored is clearly perceived as a form of rejection. Children want to be part of the action, not apart from it. This desire for involvement holds true unless, of course, they *expect* to be humiliated or rejected.

WHY FUN?

We should never lose sight of the fact that the primary reason children play games at all is to have fun. Without a sense of fun, a sense of happiness, a child can experience a joyless game. In cooperative ventures, the element of fun is enhanced as children are freed to play with others for fun, without fear of failure or rejection and without any need for destructiveness. Sharing heightens the fun experience.

When these four components are combined to create a child's game, there are no more wounded self-concepts, no more reasons for tears, no longer anything to fear. All children are freed to leave the games feeling somehow enriched by the experience. What else should a child's game be for?

games for children
three through seven

Children in this age range like lots of variety but also like to get to know a few games very well and play them over and over again. They seem to like a mix of very active and passive games, some challenging and others with very little challenge or none at all.

Even three-year-olds are perfectly capable of playing some of the games in this section and can learn how to work together as a unit if the games are broken down into very clear and simple steps. It is also interesting to note that this younger group (three through seven) is impressionable enough so that you can see, after perhaps eight weeks of directed cooperative play, spin-offs of cooperation in their other (nondirected) activity. This is something that may be harder to see in older children.

Warming Up

- *Cooperative Musical Hugs.* The kids call it Hugs, and it's a perfect warm-up exercise to open a cooperative play session. Zesty music is played while the children skip around the room. When the music stops, each child gives someone else a big hug. The music then continues, and the kids skip around again (with partners, if they want). The next time the music stops, at least three kids hug together. As the game goes on, they make a bigger and bigger hug, until finally all the children squish together in one massive musical hug. This is a wonderful way to make shy children feel good.

- *Cooperative Musical Hoops.* This is a good activity for introducing the idea of working together to very young children. The hula hoops provide a structure within which two or more children can play together, and because of this we found the hoops to be a very effective means of promoting initial cooperation among three- and four-year-olds. To begin, the group divides into pairs, with each pair standing inside a single hoop. Each child within the hoop holds up his or her portion of the hoop (usually at waist or shoulder level). Music plays while the children skip around the room, staying inside their hoop. In order to do this, the two children must move in the same direction and at the same pace. Each time the music stops, children from two different hoops team up together by stacking their hoops together and getting inside them. This process continues until as many children as possible are all together inside (and holding up) as many stacked hoops as possible. The game generally ends with about eight children in one hoop.

  Cooperative Musical Hoops can also be played *like* Cooperative Musical Chairs. In this case the hoops remain stationary on the floor and the children skip around them, jumping inside when the music stops. Each time the music stops, a hoop is removed and all the children work together to ensure that everyone (or some part of everyone) becomes part of the remaining hoop(s).

  Incidentally, if your local department store no longer has hula hoops, they can often be ordered through sporting goods stores.

- *This Is My Friend (Little People's Introduction Game).* We initially used this game to help us get to know the children's names and to help the children get to know one another's names. The game begins with the children sitting in a circle holding hands. If the children do not already know the name of the person sitting on their immediate left, they ask them. One child then kicks things off by introducing this person to the rest of the group: "This is my friend *John*." When he says

Cooperative Musical Hoops

his friend's name, he raises his friend's hand in the air. His friend then introduces the person on his left in the same way and raises her hand. This continues until everyone has been introduced and all hands are in the air, with everyone still holding hands with the friend who introduced him and the friend he introduced.

After playing this game successfully with five- and six-year-olds, we tried it with preschool children. It took five or six sessions to get it working smoothly. The children had never before introduced anyone else. Up until this time introductions had always been a "me" thing, never a "we" thing. However, once they got the hang of it, every time they came into the gym they immediately ran to a blue mat in the center of the gym and played their little intro game before moving on to other cooperative ventures. Slightly older children (five-, six-, and seven-year-olds) can move beyond the names and begin to ask their friends some simple questions to gain additional information to share with others (e.g., "This is my friend Barbara. She has a dog. She likes painting"). We have adapted this approach for use with older groups by asking them to find out as many things as possible about their new acquaintance (or something new about an old friend) in four or five minutes and then having them introduce their friend. At some workshops I start with the Little People's Introduction Game, but the adults must find out one piece of information in addition to a name.

- *Gesture Name Game.* This is another name game that is quite active and fun for smaller kids. They begin by standing in a circle. Each player in turn makes a gesture while saying each syllable in his or her name. For example, while Jane Snowshoe is saying "Jane," she raises her hand. On "Snowshoe," she stamps one foot with the first syllable and the other foot with the second syllable. Together the group then says, "Hello, Jane Snowshoe," repeating her name and gestures twice. Then it's on to the second person. The person initiating the game attempts to keep the pace quick and lively.

Easy Linking and Puzzle Games

- *Partners.* The children run, hop, skip, or twirl around the gym with a partner. The four-year-olds start by holding hands with one partner and end up linked to many partners. They like to play this game to music. The five- and six-year-olds usually start by scooting around the room on their own, and on the signal "Partners," they quickly find a nearby partner, hold hands, and "freeze" together on the spot. After dropping hands, one child then becomes a "mirror" and imitates whatever the other child does. Each partner takes a turn being the mirror. The children then run around the room again until they hear "Partners." This time each child finds a new partner. If necessary, introductions ("Howdy, partner. I'm Jane. What's your name?") can be incorporated into this game to help children get to know one another's names.

A good way to get young partners together is to cut some magazine pictures in half, hand them out, and ask the children to find their other half. This is particularly helpful in cases where some children are not chosen as partners by other children.

- *Numbers, Shapes, and Letters Together.* The children play this game with one or more partners. Ask if they can make a certain number, shape (e.g., circle, triangle, square), or letter with their bodies. How they do it is up to them, just as long as everyone in their group is a part of it.

On one occasion a group of eight four-year-olds made a circle of heads; five- and six-year-olds made beautiful 3's; and seven-year-olds made neat *X*'s and even

Numbers, Shapes, and Letters Together

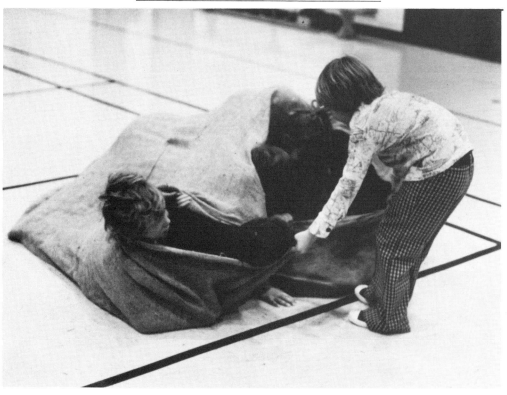

Little People's Big Sack

double *X*'s. I have found that forming numbers works very well with three little bodies. However, for most challenges the children themselves can come up with the number of bodies they need for their unique approach. Older children can join together to spell words (for example, their names) with their bodies, or can have the whole class spell a "body sentence." This "together" game can also be played in water with various age groups. The children will usually find their own way to make it work.

• *Big Turtle.* A group of about seven or eight children get on their hands and knees under a large "turtle shell" and try to make the turtle move in one direction. A gym mat works fine as a shell; use your imagination for other materials, such as a large sheet of cardboard or plastic, or a blanket, tarpaulin, or mattress.

When we first tried this with five-year-olds, the children all moved in different directions and the turtle shell dropped to the floor. But before long they realized that they had to work together to get the turtle to move. When we first tried this with four-year-olds, as soon as the shell was placed on their collective backs, the children all lay down and curled up. After carefully explaining to them that they had to stay on their hands and knees if the turtle was to move, we heaved the shell upon their backs with great gusto. They all lay down. We weren't ready to give up yet, so we tried having the turtle move around without its shell (collective crawling in one direction). This worked fine. I thought to myself . . . this time when the shell is moved into place, it's for sure going to work. It didn't! I thought about bringing in a real turtle to let the kids watch it and follow it, or making an authentic-looking turtle top out of some light stuffed material. But before I could turn these ideas into action, these little four-year-olds got the idea of Big Turtle working beautifully.

Six- and seven-year-old children can have fun trying to get the turtle to go over a mountain (a bench will do) or through an obstacle course without losing the shell. Five-year-olds also enjoy playing this game with the theme of "the tortoise and the hare"; as in the fable, the tortoise follows a straight line and the hare (three little people hopping together) zigzags all over the place.

• *Big Snake.* Did you ever see a little people's snake that wiggles and squiggles and hisses its way across the forest? If not, then you'd better let your children introduce you to Big Snake. The children start by stretching out on their stomachs and holding the ankles of the person in front of them to make a two-people snake that slithers across the floor on its belly. They soon connect up for a four-people snake, an eight-people snake, and so on, until the whole group is one Big Snake. At various lengths, the children like to see if they can turn the whole snake over on its back without its coming apart. The snake can also go over "mountains," through "holes," or up "trees," or may curl up and go to sleep. It takes a co-ordinated snake to do these last two feats. What children seem to enjoy most is getting the whole snake together.

After eight months of making a Big Snake, our kindergarten children now have a performing snake that can do tricks like rolling over and standing up.

- *Tug of Peace.* Contrary to tug of war, where teams pull against each other, Tug of Peace allows all children holding a single rope to cooperate to meet the final objective. All you need is about twenty skipping ropes and some cooperative children. The children divide into groups and attempt to create specific patterns using a rope. For example, for a triangle, three children are required to pull gently to keep the rope taut at a specific point. Different letters and shapes can be introduced that require more points or bends in the rope, which in turn encourages larger group interaction. Different groups can then join together to make more complicated patterns. Eventually all the ropes can be joined together, and the whole class can work as a cooperative team to make the shapes. In order to make this game more active, the children can run to some point before making their shape. In this case all team members maintain contact with the rope during the run (throwing it over their shoulders, circling it around them, or whatever they decide).

The difficult part of this game is overcoming the concept of "tug of war." If the children begin to pull too hard, try to direct this force toward a common goal. For example, if the children are making a triangle or a square, they can begin in a seated position and all pull hard so they can all come up to a standing position.

- *Caterpillar Over the Mountain.* First the children work together either to construct a mountain or to move it into place. The mountain can consist of a bench, large playblocks, a small boat turned upside down, or anything else that appeals to them. Once the children have helped move the mountain (which even the youngest group is fully capable of doing), they again work together to put the grass on top of the mountain. A mat draped over the mountain makes good grass.

To form the caterpillar, the children line up on their hands and knees, and hold the ankles of the child in front of them. Four children can form one sixteen-legged caterpillar, which moves around the room and over the mountain. Caterpillars can link up with other caterpillars until one giant caterpillar is formed, which crawls over the mountain and slides down the other side. A whole-class caterpillar may need more than one mountain to crawl over. Caterpillars can also coil up or crawl into a cocoon.

Little People's Big Sack

If you have the time and the creative energy, a caterpillar-like cover with a fuzzy head and lots of little sewn-on feet (and peepholes or holes for little hands to fit through) could be made, beneath or within which the children maneuver and even exchange places. This would be particularly appropriate for three-, four-, and five-year-olds. For those interested in becoming more elaborate, Chinese dragons or horses that require several children to operate them can also be used. A big colorful head with material draped behind can be many things and can even go through a human obstacle course (e.g., under human legs, over human arms, between human bellies).

• *Little People's Big Sack.* We have made several different-sized Big Sacks, which hold between eight and twenty children. They try to maneuver the sack by collective shuffling, hopping, crawling, or rolling. The first sack we made came from an old burlap canoe cover. We simply cut it up and sewed it together in the shape of a giant potato sack. The second one we made out of durable old white sheets. In both cases the sacks were light and the kids could see through the material, which guarded against anyone feeling too closed in.

One kindergarten teacher commented on how Big Sack was increasingly well received at different points in her cooperative games program:

First time: "What a delight! Half of them in the bag [big sack] trying to roll from the back of the room to the front of the room. Many squeals of delight from inside the bag. The half left out fought over who was getting in next . . . rotten crew! Mad when it was put away."

Later in program: "Today I just put the bag on the floor and said nothing. Most of them [sixteen] got in but didn't fit well (they couldn't move as a unit). Tina [five-year-old girl] organized the entire group—to get in one at a time and get closer together. 'If we work together, it's for sure going to work,' she said. It did, with only one difference of opinion."

Still later in the program: "Big sack outside on the grass—what fun! The more it's used, it appears the better they get along. There were no overt nasties."

- *Toesies.* If you are going to have a cooperative head, you might just as well have a cooperative foot. Kindergarten children giggle all the way through this one. Partners simply lie stretched out on the floor, feet to feet (or big toe to big toe), and attempt to roll across the floor keeping their toes touching throughout. Toesies can also be attempted with only the toes of the right feet connected, with legs crisscrossed, or while in a sitting (L) position, rolling toe to toe. Try it!

- *Choo-Choo Train.* The five-year-olds never seem to tire of this one. Two or more children form a train and chug around the gym maintaining contact by keeping both hands on the hips (or shoulders) of the child immediately in front of them. Cars begin to link together until there is one big train moving in unison. The conductor (teacher or child) can see if the train can go up a steep hill really slowly, swoosh down the hill, go backwards, get the cars really close together, make train noises, squat down to go through a low tunnel.

- *Beach-Ball Balance.* In this game one beach ball or balloon is shared by two children, who try to hold the ball between them without using their hands. They can see how many different ways they can balance the ball between them (head to head, side to side, stomach to stomach, back to back, and so on) and can attempt to move around the room holding the ball in different ways. With the beach ball balanced forehead to forehead, they can both attempt to bend forward to touch their knees, touch their toes, both squat down, and so on. They can then attempt to go through a hanging hoop or an obstacle course. Alternatively, they can try to balance two or three balls between them or balance the ball(s) in groups of three and four and so on.

A five-year-old boy suggested they try to balance all the balls between all the children. Naturally we tried it. They weren't totally successful but they had a lot of fun in the process.

Another variation is to have partners form a circle and see if they can pass a series of balls from one set of partners to another without using their hands, or pick up a ball (or water balloon) off the floor using heads only or backs only. Some of our six-year-old children tried to make a beach-ball train by standing in a line and placing a beach ball between each person. Many children can link up in this manner to make a big train, which moves around the gym. Some of our seven-year-olds tried to hold bean bags (which you can buy or make yourself) between their bodies while moving around the gym and through an obstacle course. This provides an interesting challenge and certainly brings the children into close contact.

Beachball Balance (Balloon Togetherness)

Games with More Movement and Motion

- *Family of Elephants.* In pairs, children create an elephant with their bodies, or by both straddling a stick that has a head (e.g., decorated paper bag) and tail (rope) attached to it. Human arms make fine elephant trunks. Elephants plod or gallop around the room, connecting trunks (arms) to tails (ropes), until the whole family is linked together.

Secret messages, consisting of pictures of a certain number of elephants connected together, can be placed around the room. The children can show or share these messages with other elephants and then attempt to follow the picture (message).

- *Wagon Wheels.* The wagon wheel is created by about seven children facing each other and joining hands to make a circle. The wheel then moves in a circular motion around the walls of the gym. Two or three children (the bottom of the wheel) have their backs touching the wall momentarily as the wheel spins along the wall.

The fun increases as the wheel picks up speed. As a six-year-old said to me, "It wheely works!" Try putting it into reverse or changing the speed limit for more fun. The wheel can stop by turning itself into a human hubcap. To do this, one child lets go of her wheelmate's hand and begins to turn toward the inside of the circle, drawing the line into the center. This coiling process continues until everyone, still holding hands, is wrapped into a human hub.

- *Double Bubble.* Bubbles are formed by two or three children holding hands or using any other means the children devise to make a small circle. The bubbles begin by floating around slowly, being careful not to bump in to any other bubbles for fear of being popped. The object of the game is for the children to work together to create their bubble and to avoid collision. The bubbles can hop, bop, or twirl around once the children become familiar with the game.

To vary the game, children in groups of two or three are still bubbles but the objective becomes to merge the little bubble into bigger bubbles. This can be done by two two-people bubbles gently squeezing together until the bubble pops into a four-people bubble. This process continues until there is only one giant bubble. Again, music can add extra fun to this game.

Action Games

- *Frozen Bean Bag (Help Your Friends).* This is an active game of helping. All the children begin by moving around the gym at their own pace, each balancing a bean bag on his or her head. The leader or teacher can change the action or pace by asking the children to try to skip, hop, go backwards, go slower, go faster, etc. If the bean bag falls off a child's head, he or she is frozen. Another child must then pick up the bean bag and place it back on the frozen player's head to free him, without losing his own bean bag. The object of the game is to help your friends by keeping them unfrozen. At the end of the game the children can be asked, how many people helped their friends, or how many times did you help your friends? If desired, a quick count of helping acts can be taken. This is a good game for six-, seven-, and eight-year-olds, and can be a lot of fun when played to music. Five-year-olds can hold on to their own bean bag while helping another, rather than balancing it on their heads.

- *Sticky Popcorn.* The children begin this game by "popping"—jumping or hopping—about the gym as individual pieces of sticky popcorn, searching for other pieces of popcorn. When one piece of popcorn comes into contact with another piece, they stick together. Once stuck, they continue to pop around together, sticking to other pieces, until they all end up in a big popcorn ball.

  From our experience with five-year-olds, be forewarned that sticky popcorn balls will begin to pop up at the strangest times—on the way down to the gym or while children are in the process of getting their coats off after recess. They can also merely "pop corn" in a group by forming a tightly knit circle with their arms around each other (or hand in hand). Several popping balls (from three to twenty-three soccer-type balls) are placed inside the circle, and the children move around as a unit, trying to keep the balls inside.

- *Bridges.* Bridges, bridges, and more bridges. How many kinds of bridges can be built? You'll need a bean bag and a stick 2 to 3 inches wide for every two children. First the children link benches together to set up a series of bridges reaching across the gym. Next they pass the equipment down the line from one to another so that the first person to get to the equipment holder has the honor of being first passer and last to get his or her own equipment. When each child has a partner and each set of partners has a bean bag and a stick, they are ready to begin. Each child takes one end of the stick, and the two partners try to balance their bean bag in the middle of the stick between them while moving around the gym. Generally the children face each other and begin by following the lines on the

Caterpillar Over the Mountain

Big Snake

Balance Beam Progression

floor, which lead them to the various bridges. Soon they climb up onto the first bridge, trying to keep the stick level and the bean bag in balance. As they approach the end of the bench, the person walking forward tells his partner (who is walking backwards) that the end of the bench is coming. ("Be careful . . . step down.") This is an important time to develop concern for the other child's welfare. A variation of "bean-bag" bridges is to have the children go through the course (a) in pairs, balancing a ball between them using two sticks ("ball bridges"), or (b) in fours, balancing a cup of water on a stiff paper plate with four sticks. To build less tangible, personal bridges is the ultimate aim.

● *Magic Carpet.* A group of about seven children take turns giving each other magic-carpet rides on a gym mat. With kindergarten children the middle person's "ride" can consist of getting "jiggled" around in one spot, which they all seem to enjoy. In some cases the "carpet" is pulled steadily to the other side of the gym, with the middle person lying, sitting, or crouching on the mat. The rider can choose the riding position and can control the speed ("slower," "faster," "just right"). In the beginning, a rotation for taking turns could be suggested or it can occur spontaneously, depending upon the group.

- *Fish Gobbler.* A big favorite! Five- and six-year-old kids really love this one. All you need is an area big enough for all the children to spread out with ample room to maneuver. When the caller (known as the Fish Gobbler) shouts "Ship," all the children run toward the wall to which he points. On the shout "Shore," they quickly change directions and run toward the opposite wall. On the signal "Fish Gobbler," the kids quickly drop to the floor on their stomachs and link arms, legs, or bodies together with one or more friends. The Fish Gobbler moves around the room with arms outstretched like a big bird swimming toward the other players but not touching any of them. The children are all "safe" as long as they are all physically linked together. Once the Fish Gobbler sees that everyone is linked to someone else, the signal "Rescue" is called. At this moment all the children jump to their feet, join hands, and yell "Yah," raising their joined hands over their heads. The game ends when the children are ready to move on to another game. Various other calls could be added, such as "Sardines" (everyone runs to a central point to make the tightest group possible by either lying on the floor or forming a massive standing hug); "Fishermen All" (everyone sits on someone else's knee or knees); "Crabs" (everyone backs up to a partner, bends over, and reaches under their own legs to hold hands); "Fishnet" (let the kids use their imagination and decide how to make one).

- *Grasshopper.* The name of the game came from a six-year-old girl, who thought it was definitely a grasshopper. See what you think. About eight or ten children arrange themselves standing around the edges of a sturdy blanket. A beach ball (grasshopper) is placed in the center of the blanket, and the children try to make it hop. It takes a collective effort to get that grasshopper high in the air and then back onto the blanket, without letting the grasshopper fall on the floor. It usually takes five-year-olds several sessions to get the hang (or hop) of this, particularly moving as a unit to catch the ball, but they do get it. It's fun, and the grasshopper can do other things, too, like rolling around the outside edge of the blanket, just missing everyone's fingers (where they hold on to the blanket). For added excitement and challenge, cut a hole in the center of the blanket, big enough for a beach ball or balloon to pass through. See if the kids can get the grasshopper to roll through the hole or jump into the air and come down through the hole. This works with a parachute, too.

- *Parachute.* The canopy (umbrella-like portion) of an old parachute provides still another means of inflating the cooperative spirit. The players spread themselves around the chute, grasping hold of its edge. The chute is inflated by everyone lifting arms over head in unison. Once the chute is inflated, the children can walk beneath it toward the center still holding on to the edges, meet in the center under the chute, and then walk back out to their original positions. While the players are all in the center under the inflated chute, they can also all let go of the chute at the same time and freeze in place while the chute falls down on them. (Signals such as "Walk," "Out," "Let go," can be given aloud, if desired.) Players can be prepared for "letting go" together by having them hold on to the edge of the chute while it is on the floor (pulling it tight) and releasing on the signal. If the chute is released at the same time, it will spring evenly toward the center. The children may have to practice this a few times until everyone lets go at the same time.

In another chute game each player is given a number from 1 to 5 (or each group of children choose a name for themselves). Players stand around the chute holding it at waist level, and as their number (or group name) is called, each member of that group lies on the ground face up under the chute in the form of a star (like upside-down skydivers linked together). The remaining players shake the chute

Frozen Bean Bag

up and down on them for a minute or so, giving them an air wave. Parachute activities can begin with very young children and continue through virtually all age ranges.

For five-year-olds, the parachute was one of the best motivators for cooperation. The children really had to work together to get the puffy results they wanted. One teacher commented that the destructively aggressive children were unusually calm and gentle when handling the silk. It was one of our best cooperative ventures.

If you have trouble getting hold of an old parachute from a skydiving club, military outpost, or surplus store, you might try sewing together a few sheets or light nylon sails leaving a hole in the middle (for air to get through).

- *Mile of Yarn.* This is an interesting way to knit young children together. One child starts with a bright ball of thick yarn (or a strip of material), wraps the end of the yarn around her waist, and passes the ball to another child. He wraps it around his waist, and passes it to another child, and so on. Once the whole group has been intertwined in yarn, the whole process is reversed. The last player begins to rewind the ball, passes it to the next child, and so on until the fully wound ball reaches the first child.

- *Lasso—Hee Ha.* The group is divided, half into "partners" and half "horses." All the children (partners and horses) work together to get a thick rope around about half of the group (horses). The rope is tied or braided together at one end so that it forms a circle (like a large lasso). Once all the horses are inside the lasso, they all hold on to the rope surrounding them and spin in the same direction. They try to get the trailing portion of the rope to spin in a circular manner so the rest of the children can jump over the rope with their partner as it passes by. Partners and horses then switch positions.

With one group of kindergarten children, we never could get this game to work "properly" (per these instructions), but the kids loved it anyway. The group in the lasso ran, the rest ran after them to try to catch the trailing rope. When this was achieved, they all fell down in a heap, laughing hysterically. Older children seem to be better able to make the game work in the way described above—but either way, everyone has fun.

- *Blup-Blup-up-up.* This is a good game to introduce children to the idea of a collective score. (See pages 50–56 for many more collective-score games.) Pairs of children try to keep a balloon up in the air by taking turns hitting it. They can count the number of consecutive hits, and if the balloon hits the ground, they just pick it up and continue counting from the point where they left off or start counting over again. The game can also be played in small groups of three or four with each child taking a turn, and in different formations (circle, square).

For additional challenge and excitement, two or more children can attempt to keep a balloon up outdoors with the aid of implements such as water shooters. They can also just blow on the balloon.

For a collective effort without a collective score, partners or groups of three can work together trying to keep a balloon up with alternate hand hits (or with water shooters) while going from one end of the field to the other or while going through an obstacle course (over walls, through tunnels, etc.)

Games for Rainy Days

These games rely more on imagination than on movement, and are perfect for indoors, when you would like to play a quieter game. Of course, there's no reason not to play them when the sun is shining brightly, too!

• *Barnyard.* Each player selects an animal name or animal picture out of a hat, or someone (leader) whispers the name of one of two or three different animals to different players. For example, to end up with three groups you might whisper either "cow," "wolf," or "snake" to each player. The players then scatter themselves around the room and shut their eyes, put on blindfolds, or in some way turn out the lights for the animal action. Some kids have even played it with their eyes wide open. The object of the game is to find all the members of your specific animal group and to link arms with them. The only means of communication allowed is your animal sound.

You can create many variations to this game. For example, stipulate that each group should end up with three cows, three snakes, and three wolves. Groups of different animals can all link together, and then as a group find the sleeping, snoring farmer or the little lost sheep (who are stationary but can make soft sounds). Each group of animals can also find their "den," which can be designated by a stuffed animal, a large mat, or a rope.

For other alternatives—such as with eyes open and voices silent—each person can imitate his animal and claim as his mate or mates other people imitating the same animal. Pairs or groups of similar animals can link up and move around the gym together as if they were one animal. Each group can guess what the other groups of animals are.

When we played this game one spring day, we added a group of frogs. Soon two

Cleaning Up Together

groups of frogs seemed to have formed, and with all the seriousness a five-year-old could muster, a small friend said, "We better decide if a frog goes 'ribbit' or 'croak.'"

●　*Blizzard.*　With practice, this game creates excellent communication between children. Two children are lost in a snowstorm (or sandstorm) and are trying to get back home. One of the children is "snow-blind" and the other can see. The objective is to lead the snow-blind friend (who has his eyes shut or is blindfolded) through the blizzard (obstacle course) to safety. In pairs, the children go through a snow tunnel (hoop), under an ice log (bench), over a partially frozen river (small mat), and across a snow bridge (bench). Partners hold hands or link arms and try not to let go "so no one gets lost alone in the storm." Once they reach "safety," the partners can switch roles.

One kindergarten teacher commented, "My children love this one and have real empathy for the blind person. Once the stage is set, they demonstrate a gentleness that I don't see in other games."

For additional challenge (or older groups) the children can attempt to direct their partner through the course safely by talking to her, by singing to her, or by a special code other than talking or holding hands (for example, clap hands to move one way; tap on shoulder to step up; or snap finger, hum, or use a musical instrument for special instructions). Children can also lead their partner around a pool (in water) by a code the two have devised, or without speaking try to teach their partner to do some designated task. For kids who like more "modern" plots, the blizzard story could be changed to something like "control tower to pilot." The pilot cannot see because of heavy fog. The objective is for the controller to direct the pilot safely through various obstacles and onto the runway.

• *Electronic People Machine.* This is a game that takes no equipment except a very active imagination. The children pretend that they are all parts of an electronic machine and must work together for the machine to run. The kind of machine they form—whether real, like a computer or automobile, or totally imaginary—is up to them, as is how they each take part. The machine "turns on" when music is played, and starts to move its parts, which are the legs, head, hands, and hips of the players. When the music stops, the machine stops. If you need a little more structure to get the machine tuned up, all the children can hold hands and form a line, making a simple moving machine. Every other child can be asked to bend his or her trunk forward while the rest of the children bend their trunks backward, or to squat down when the others all stand up, or to all raise their left leg up and down, and so on.

The children can also pretend to be a smiling machine or a laughing machine with everyone smiling and laughing, or some can become a tickling machine, which the other children go through at will. Older kids might try making a more complicated machine, like a human pinball machine.

• *Jigsaw-Puzzle People and Animals.* Everybody works together to turn different bodies into different parts of a newly created animal (or giant person). To begin with, a specific animal can be suggested, body parts can be proposed, or each child can select a card on which he has drawn a picture of a different body part. The children then proceed to team up with other parts to make a total being. Once children are familiar with this activity, they can merely be asked to make any kind of animal they want with two or more friends. They will make all sorts of things—horses, elephants, gorillas, even octopuses. On one occasion a horse transformed into an octopus right before my eyes, "so everyone could have a part." You never know precisely what the creation will look like, but everyone will be a part of it and the children can tell you exactly what it is.

Once each group has formed its animal, see if they can get it to move, kneel, or lie down, curl up, stretch out, wag its tail, and so on.

Another approach is to let the children "make a person." What they will be doing, in effect, is creating a life-size paper puppet from their own body parts. This works best in groups of six. First, the children divide into pairs, each pair choosing one set of body parts (arms, legs, trunk, and head) as their own. Each child then traces his or her partner's actual designated body part on a long piece of paper. They then help each other cut out the parts, each starting by cutting at a different end. Next the group puts all six body parts together on the floor or on the wall, using masking tape, to make one collective human being.

- *Shoe Twister.*   Each child removes one shoe and places it in a pile. Everyone then picks up someone else's shoe, and while holding the shoe (method left up to children's ingenuity) everyone joins hands, forming a large circle. Each child then locates the owner of the shoe that she is holding, and all children exchange shoes *without breaking their joined hands.* Once all shoes have been returned to their owners, the circle is reformed and children make another pile of shoes to start the game again.

- *Tiptoe Through the Tulips.*   The children work together to create (construct, paint, cut out, or paste on) a lovely lane of tulips through which they can tiptoe. You'll need a long sheet of white, brown, or colored construction paper, bowls of three or four different water-color paints, and some paint brushes. Then you bring on the kids and the real fun begins! The children paint a long winding lane of flowers and leaves—and if they like, also paint one anothers' toes—with the brightly colored paints, and "tiptoe through the tulips." Once the collective creation is completed, the children hang the mural together. This can get a little messy. You might want to play this game outside on some unexpected bright spring day, with singing and music, too.

- *Secret Message (Telephone).*   Secret messages still have great intrigue for five-year-olds. In this game all the children sit close together in a tight circle and pass whispers or signs. A parent, teacher, or child selects a word or short phrase and whispers it into the ear of the person on the right (for example, "I like you"). The secret is passed on to the next person until everyone has received the message. Messages can be passed around faster and faster to add to the fun. The last person then says the message out loud and the children compare it to the original secret. The same phrase (or different phrases) can be started in both directions. The children can also pass friendly "signs," such as a happy face, a warm hug, a gentle squeeze, a handshake, a snuggle, or a wink.

This quiet game is a good "gearing down" activity. It's amazing how even five-year-olds are attentive, curious to hear how the message will "turn out."

Old Games, New Ways

You may find it easier to introduce the idea of cooperation through games that are already familiar to the children. Here are some nonelimination versions of three traditional favorites; you can see from them how simple it is to adapt standard competitive games for cooperative fun!

- *Hot Potato.* The children join hands and sit down to form a potato-passing circle. A hot potato (bean bag or ball) is passed around the circle from one person to the next until the potato caller (who is outside the circle facing the other way) yells, "Hot potato!" The person with the potato in his or her hands at this time joins a separate "potato-callers" circle and chooses a number, to which the callers count softly together before yelling "Hot potato!" in unison. The game continues in this manner until the last child has switched to the potato-callers circle and all the other children have had a chance to select a "hot potato" number to count to. It is interesting to note that the children have no sense of losing in this game. They enjoy being in either circle, as both circles are "in."

- *Nonelimination Simon Says.* Two games begin simultaneously, each with a leader, who performs various movements which the children mimic when given the command "Simon says do this." However, when the leader says, "Do this," without first having said, "Simon says," any child who follows merely transfers to the second game, joining in the next time "Simon Says" instead of being eliminated, as in the traditional game. In this way there is no exclusion, only movement back and forth between two parallel games. Nonelimination Simon Says can also be played in pairs. Why Simon never said, "No one will be left out" before now is beyond me.

- *Nonelimination Musical Chairs.* The object is to keep everyone in the game even though chairs are systematically removed. As in the competitive version, music is played, and more and more chairs are removed each time the music stops. In this game, though, more and more children have to team up together, sitting on parts of chairs or on each other to keep everyone in the game. In the end, all twenty children who started the game are delicately perched on one chair, as opposed to nineteen disappointed children standing on the sidelines with one "winner" on one chair.

If you happen to play this game in a park and there are no chairs available, people on their hands and knees can serve as singing chairs. Together they can decide when their music will stop, and as human chairs are removed, they merely join the other group (sitting).

Partner Gymnastics

There are a great number of gymnastic stunts that can be executed only with one or more partners—for example, pyramids, balancing stunts, double rolls, triple rolls, foot pitches, teeter-board stunts, even the flying trapeze. See the Recommended Reading on page 121 for a good gymnastics book on stunts and tumbling or a comprehensive elementary physical-education book with a wide selection to choose from. A few simple cooperative stunts for young children are presented below.

- *Partner Pull-up.* Partners sit down facing each other with the soles of their feet on the floor, toes touching. Partners reach forward, bending their knees if they must, and grasp hands. By pulling together, both come up to a stand and then try to return to a sitting position. Pull-up can also be done in groups.

- *Partner Back-up.* Two children sit back to back, knees bent. From this position they try to stand up by pushing against each other's backs without moving their feet. Sitting down again can also be attempted. If the children are successful, propose that from a halfway position they try to move like a spider. Back-up can be done in groups of threes, fours, or fives.

- *Wring the Dishrag.* Two children stand facing each other and join right hands (as if shaking hands). Player 1 swings his right leg over the head of Player 2, taking a straddle position over his own arm. Player 2 swings her left leg over Player 1. The partners are now back to back (actually behind to behind). Player 1 continues by bringing his left leg over and faces in the original direction. Player 2 swings her right leg over to the original face-to-face position. It may sound complicated but it's really quite simple. Grab someone and try it . . . you'll see.

- *Hop-along.* Partners stand facing each other. Both raise their left leg straight out, high enough for their partner to grasp hold of their ankle. Once they can balance each other in this position, partners can try to hop along (to the market, to the store) or may even try to lower themselves down to the floor. Coming back up is a little tougher and may require the help of a few more friends.

Singing Games

Cooperative songs can be used for more fun in game-playing. Here are a few singing games we've enjoyed playing, but you can adapt the lyrics to songs that your children know. In the latter three cooperative singing games there is only intermittent active involvement. However, the kids like them and that is a crucial test.

- *The More We Get Together.*   The children begin the game by skipping around the gym, hand in hand, with one or two partners, singing:

> The more we get together,
> Together, together.
> The more we get together,
> The happier we'll be.
> For your friends are my friends,
> And my friends are your friends;
> The more we get together,
> The happier we'll be.

Every time they sing "together," more friends join together, until everyone is holding hands. At the end of the song all the children form a circle and rush to the middle of the circle, raising their hands way up in the air and cheering.

- *The Big Ship Sails.*   All the children hold hands and form a circle. Two children form the prow of the ship, one holding on to the other's waist from behind. Weaving in and out of the circle, they repeatedly go under the raised arms of the other children as all sing this song:

> Oh, the big ship sails through
> The alley alley o, the alley alley o,
> The alley alley o.
> Oh, the big ship sails through
> The alley alley o,
> Heigh ho alley alley o.

When the verse stops at "Heigh ho alley alley o," the ship also stops, and the two children with arms raised closest to the end of the ship join on to the back of the ship. The smaller circle reconnects and the bigger ship weaves in and out again as the children sing the song. The ship continues to get bigger in this manner until finally all children are part of the big ship, and they then sail around the room taking short snappy steps and singing.

- *Thread the Needle.* A single line of about eight children joins hands. The first child is the needle and begins by leading the line (thread) under the raised arms of the last two children (seventh and eighth), singing:

> The thread follows the needle,
> The thread follows the needle.
> In and out the needle goes
> As we mend the clothes.

The seventh child ends up facing the eighth with his arms crossed in front of him. This forms the first stitch. The needle then continues in the same direction and leads the line under the arms of the sixth and seventh children, which forms another stitch. This is repeated until the entire line has been stitched, with the leader turning under her own arm to complete the last stitch. To "rip" the stitch, the children raise their arms overhead, still holding hands, and turn back to their original positions. The eighth child now moves to the front of the line to become the new needle. Continue until everyone has had a turn as needle.

- *Here We Come Walking.*

1. Here we come walking
   Down the street, down the street.
   Here we come walking down the street.
   How are you today?

2. Here we come knocking
   At your door, at your door.
   Here we come knocking at your door.
   Come outside and play.

3. La la la la la la,
   La la la, la la la,
   La la la la la la, la la la,
   La la la la la.

The children join hands, form a circle large enough for children to skip around inside, and sit down. To the first verse of the song several children begin by walking hand in hand down the imaginary street inside the circle. On the second verse they release their handhold to go and knock at a friend's imaginary door (tap on floor in front of a friend). They help their new friend up by taking his or her hand, and all players in the middle of the circle join hands and skip around to the third verse. This procedure continues until everyone has come out to play, with the number doubling each time they go knocking at the doors.

Can You Do Things Together?

This game has an infinite number of variations. The common thread running through the different activities is that children must achieve the objective by performing the task or acting out the motion with one or more friends together.

Can you walk through a field of sticky glue with your partner?

Can you swim through Jell-O with your partner?

Can you be real tall with your partner?

Can you be real small with your partner?

Can you be one frog with your partner?

Can you do a round thing with your friend while holding his or her hand?

Can you bounce your partner like a ball?

Can you and your partner hold hands and saw wood together like lumberjacks?

Can you make a human chair for your partner to sit on? A two-people chair? A four-people chair?

Can you skip around with three friends?

Can you get behind your partner, wrap your arms around his front, and walk at the same time as he does? Can four people do it?

Can you make a fort with your friends and all get inside it?

Can you go through an obstacle course (e.g., under bench, through hoop, across beam) without letting go of your partner's hand?

Can you make a people tunnel that someone can go through? Can you take turns going through the tunnel but keep the tunnel as long as possible?

Can you find your partner's heartbeat? After a quiet game? After an active game?

Can you each get a stick (or broom) and together with a partner try to bounce and catch a beach ball using both your sticks?

Can you get in groups of three or four and see if you can carry a beach ball across the gym holding it way over your heads with floor-hockey sticks or brooms?

With your back stuck to your partner's back, can you move around the gym? Jump forward toward this wall? Jump backwards toward this wall? Both get inside a hoop and move around still stuck back to back?

Can you roll a big hula hoop on its edge so your partner can run through it?

Can your partner roll it so you can run through it?

Can you make a people sandwich with four or five friends? (e.g., with ham, lettuce, mustard, and 2 slices of bread)

Can you sit down across from your friend, feet to feet, and row a boat?

Can you roll your partner(s) like a log? Can you jump over your log(s)? Can you drag your log(s) across the floor? Can you (and a friend) stand your log up like a telephone pole?

Can you think of some other neat things to do together?

Cleaning Up Together

- *Bull's Eye.* This can be a fun way to put equipment away cooperatively at the end of a session of game-playing. The children lift a bench together and carry the bench through one or more hula hoops. All the children also go through the hoop, including the ones holding the hoop(s). When this is played with several hoops, the kids might like to go inside some hoops and outside others.

- *Eco-Ball.* This game introduces an important concept of cooperation, not only with one another but with the natural environment. After a cooperative games day, the game site is divided into different sections. Each team is given a garbage bag (or two) and is responsible for cleaning up their section. The common goal is for everyone to work together to have *all* litter picked up, in or out of their area. A collective scoring system can be introduced if desired—for example, one point for each piece of litter that originated with the games day and two points for litter that was there before.

games for children
eight through twelve

As with the previous games, there is nothing sacred about the age category suggested for this chapter. Though we tested most of these games with children of these ages and found them well received, some of the games presented (such as Log Roll) are perfectly acceptable for six-year-olds and sixty-year-olds. Others (such as Collective Blanketball games) are well received by children, teen-agers, and adults with youthful outlooks, whatever their age. So stay flexible and open-minded when thinking about how to use the games and with whom.

Introducing Cooperative Ideas

The first two games here show how easy it is to remake an old game into a new, sharing one. From there on, kids will take the cue from you!

Balloon Bucket

● *Frozen Tag.* If you want to play a tag game, why not introduce some helping components? A few children are designated "freezers" while the rest of the children scatter in all directions. The freezers count to ten, and then take off after the runners. When a child is tagged, he freezes in a stride position or with a hand extended. To unfreeze him, another child must either pass under his legs or shake his hand. The number of freezers can be adjusted to keep the game moving. When the children are tired or ready to play something else, the leader can ask the children, "How many of you unfroze your friends?"

Frozen Tag can also be played in pairs with twin freezers, twin runners, twin freezes, and twin unfreezers. Partners hold hands and run together, freeze together, and unfreeze together, with *both* partners shaking hands with the frozen pair or going under the frozen pair's legs. It can also be played in groups of three, and in shallow water, where children swim under each other's legs to unfreeze each other.

● *Hug Tag.* This is another cooperative variation of "regular" tag. A player is safe from being tagged only when she is hugging another player. For more hugging, propose that only three children hugging together are safe, then four, then five, and so on. Younger children really enjoy this game.

- *Human Tangles.* The following two games attempt to bring people together by having them work as a unit to untangle themselves. In Human Knots about ten players stand in a circle, place their hands in the center, and take hold of the hands of two people other than those immediately next to them. Now the group works together in an attempt to untie the knot without releasing handholds.

For the Human Pretzel all but two players hold hands in a circle and twist themselves over and under and through one another without dropping hands. The two other people, who have had their backs turned to the pretzel-making process, then try to untangle the group. The pretzel cooperates as the untanglers try to figure out who and what goes where and how.

These untangling games have been played in shallow water, where they more closely resemble human spaghetti.

- *Long, Long, Long Jump.* As the name implies, the objective of this activity is for a group of children to jump collectively as far as possible. The first player begins at a starting line and makes one jump. The next player starts his jump where the previous person landed. The players can attempt to better their total collective distance on successive tries. This can be played indoors or out, with backward broad jump, forward broad jump (standing or running), hop-skip-and-jump, and so on.

- *Watermelon Split.* If you want an active way to split up a watermelon or to work up a thirst before eating it—while encouraging some sharing initiatives—this may be the way. A whole watermelon is transported from one point to another in a relay fashion. It can be carried in a variety of fashions (alone or with partners) before being handed off or tossed to fellow carriers. The important thing is for the players to work out their own plan to accomplish the goal together. Once the watermelon has been through the course, it is cut up and shared by all watermeloners. I'm sure you can think of some cooperative venture for the watermelon pits, such as a progressive or collective watermelon pit spit.

- *Cherry Bowl.* A fruitful game for a picnic, party, or play day. Each player begins with about ten cherry pits or stones. A shallow hole is made in the ground or a shallow bowl is placed on the ground. One cherry pit is put into the shallow hole (or bowl) and each player takes a turn trying to knock it out with his cherry pit. Every time the pit is knocked out, every player gets to eat a cherry from a common supply. You can also fill the bowl with twenty cherry pits and have each player try to knock out as many as possible. If two (or three) are knocked out, then each player gets two (or three) cherries to eat, and so on until the bowl is empty.

- *Push 'Em Into Balance.* In traditional push-'em-out-of-balance games, two players face each other, grasp one or both hands, and try to push the other person off balance. If a person moves either foot, he loses. Push 'Em Into Balance games reverse this process.

Two partners face each other, place the palms of their hands together, and take one step (or several steps) backward so that they are leaning on each other to maintain balance. Then, in unison, they attempt to push each other back into balance (that is, back up into standing position) without moving their feet. The maneuver resembles a standing or leaning push-up done on a mirror, if you can visualize that. You have to be careful that your feet are secure on the floor so you don't slip. Some children like to begin this game on their knees (rebounding while kneeling), gradually moving farther and farther apart and rebounding back up to an upright position on their knees. They can also try to come to a standing position from their knees by leaning into each other and pushing up from there.

As an additional challenge they can try Partner-back-up Twirl. Players begin seated back to back, with their knees bent. By pushing against each other's back, they come about halfway up to a stand, and then, still leaning on each other to maintain balance, they rotate, turn, or roll around to a leaning front-to-front position ready for a series of standing rebounds. For those particularly "well balanced," many of these feats can be attempted atop a bench or balance beam.

- *Log Roll.* A series of logs (players) lie side by side on their stomachs on the floor, a mat, a rug, the grass, or any other comfortable surface. A rider lies on his or her stomach perpendicular to the logs, across the upper portion of their backs. All the logs then begin rolling in the same direction, giving their rider a sometimes soft, sometimes bumpy, ride across the top. Once the rider has flopped over the last log, she becomes a rolling log at the end of the line of logs. The first log to roll out from beneath the rider becomes the next rider, and is propelled across the log line. This continues until they roll out of space or until they feel like stopping.

If a larger log would prefer not to take the ride, he can just "pass" and log on. A heavy rider on light logs should go slowly and support some of his own weight

Human Supports

Circle of Friends

along the way. Two lightweight riders can try going across the rolling logs side by side. You might also want to try two lines of logs with two riders. The stretched-out logs hold hands between lines as they roll. Once it gets rolling, it's a fun game for young and old alike.

- *Circle of Friends.* In this game you literally fall into the hands of your friends, who prevent you from hitting the floor. About eight children kneel down (or stand) and form a tight circle, shoulder to shoulder. The person standing in the middle of the circle stiffens her body and falls in any direction. Generally the middle person keeps her arms "glued" to her sides and is encouraged to not move her feet. This game helps develop trust, as the people forming the circle learn to work together to catch the middle person in their hands and gently shove her in another direction. Children take turns in the middle. As proficiency increases, it is possible to back the circle up a bit (more room to fall).

Relay and Carrying Games

- *Towering Tower.* The object of this game is to have children work together to build a single tower out of bean bags, cardboard boxes, hoops, balls, old shoes, or any other materials you have handy. To have all the players actively involved all the time, the children can run (skip, hop, crabwalk, etc.) around the gym until the leader calls, "Tower!" At this point, each child gets one piece of equipment of his or her choice from a common supply and places it in the middle of the gym to help build the tower. The children then run around until "Tower!" is called again, and then add further material to the towering tower.

I remember one of the first times we played this game with a group of eight-year-olds. Just before the dismissal bell rang, they managed to place the last block on their towering tower, which had a distinct lean to it. All the children jumped up and down, cheering. I wondered, How many would have cheered if it had been a relay race?

In another approach, ask the children to select a partner or partners when "Tower!" is called, and select and carry a piece of equipment to the tower site together. If you're using large building blocks, this is functional and maybe necessary. If you're not, try having the children carry the building blocks balanced on two sticks or held between their bodies. Each time "Tower!" is called, players can select a new partner to work with.

For additional challenge, consider using very large cardboard boxes, which you can get from appliance or grocery stores. The question will be, How are we going to get this way up there? They'll find a way.

- *Over and Over.*   Players form two lines, about four and a half kid-lengths apart. The first person in each line has a beach ball (or medicine ball), which is passed backward over his or her head to the next person in line. The lead person immediately turns around and shakes (or slaps) hands with the second person ("gimme five"), who must momentarily free one hand from the ball, balancing it with the other. The lead person then runs to the end of the second, adjoining line, where another ball is being passed along. The second person repeats this procedure, and so it goes over and over down the line. The common objective is to move both balls and both lines from one point to another as quickly as possible, perhaps from one end of the gym to the other

Is variety possible in Over and Over? Sure. Two double lines are formed and partners use their *inside arms only* to pass the ball over their heads to the next set of partners, or partners lie on their backs side by side and use their *inside legs only* to pass a beach ball over their heads to the set of partners behind. The handshake is optional in this one. If the ball drops, just pick it up (with your hands) and continue from where you left off.

Another variation of Over and Over, called Under and Under, is played in water but without a ball. Players line up waist deep in water with their legs spread apart. The player who is last in line begins the game by swimming under the legs of the players in front of him. He surfaces for air whenever necessary but finally comes up at the front of the line. The person who is now last in line swims under and under, and so on up the line.

- *Square Ball.*   It's not the ball that's square, or the children. Square Ball is played by four children working as a unit to keep a rope taut in the shape of a square while each child, in turn, attempts to move the ball with his feet from a designated center spot to his corner spot and return it to the center.

For Running Square Ball, groups of four with ropes are scattered around the playing area at different bases. Each group of four kicks their ball to the next station, drops it off, and runs back to their station to get the ball that was dropped off. In order to do this, the children must move the ball while keeping it within the confines of their taut rope. This process continues until each group has its original ball back. If you want to, you can record the time it takes for *all balls* to complete the circuit.

Balance Beam Progression

Log Roll

Partner Acrobatics

Ladder Travel

- *Fruit-Cocktail Mélange.* Bananas, apples, oranges, grapefruits, melons, grapes, or any other kinds of fruit are shared in this tasteful game. Pieces of fruit are placed at one end of an open grassy area, and the players carry or roll the fruit to a mixing area at the other end. Any number of people can work together to get the fruit to the mixing area, and they can do it any way they want as long as they don't use their hands, feet, or mouths. For example, a bunch of grapes or an apple may be balanced on one bent-over back or between three people's fronts. Only when the fruit reaches the mixing area can it be eaten. Then players divide it up and enjoy eating it together, so that each team member gets a taste of each type of fruit. If you're near a lake, you might consider Floating Fruit Cocktail, where the fruit is nudged along in the water.

- *Water Exchange.* For a refreshing spray on a hot, sunny day, give Water-Cup Pass or Water-Balloon Toss a whirl. For Water-Cup Pass players stand in a circle with an empty paper cup in their teeth. One player's cup is filled with water. This person begins by pouring her water into the cup of the next person without using her hands. He then pours it into the next person's cup. This water-passing process continues all the way around the circle. For more involvement more players can start with filled cups or smaller circles can be formed. For Water-Balloon Toss partners start standing about 3 feet apart and toss a small balloon filled with water back and forth. After each round (two tosses), partners take a step backward. If the balloon bursts and you get soaked, naturally you will want to share this with your partner. Just give him or her a big hug.

- *Carry On.* Four players and one beach ball start at each base. The total number of bases depends upon the number of players. Two players from each base attempt to move their beach ball to the next base with their bodies without the use of their hands and without kicking the ball (e.g., hip to hip or stomach to back). They then pass the ball to the set of partners remaining at the next base (without using their hands), await the delivery of another ball from their partners behind them, and continue around the bases.

For something a little more strenuous, teams of three or five are formed at various equally spaced bases. The object is to get all players from one base to the next by carrying them. If three players start on each base, two of them carry the other person (Player 1) to the next base and then run back to their starting point (home base). The newly delivered person at their home base helps carry their second team member to the next base. On the next delivery their third team member will be dropped off by two team members who moved up from the base behind them. This process continues until members of all teams have been moved to another base. If you want to, you can try to have the entire class (all teams) change bases as quickly as possible. It's a fun game and can be played in snow or mud for additional messy fun and challenge.

- *Shake the Snake.* The children divide themselves into two groups: shakers and stompers. The shakers each hold the end of an 8-foot rope between their thumb and first finger and squiggle the rope, so that the end of it drags along the floor. Shakers must be running around the room while shaking the rope. The stompers try to step on the rope, thereby pulling it from between the shakers' fingers. Once a stomper has stepped on a rope and it has fallen to the floor, he or she picks it up and becomes a shaker. The shaker dropping the rope becomes a stomper. If necessary, there can be more stompers than shakers.

- *Esti-Win.* This is a strategy that changes the focus of "winning" from the fastest to the one who best knows his or her running self. Each person estimates the time it will take her to complete the distance and sees how close she comes to her prediction. Runners try to improve upon their past estimates—another way of winning.

- *Candle Carry.* Here's a relay that favors those with a moderate pace. A lighted candle is carried through a course and passed from payer to player while tricycling, bicycling, swimming, or jogging. Too swift a pace may extinguish the flame and too slow a pace may result in the flame extinguishing itself (running out of candle).

- *Cross-Over Dodgeball.* As in regular dodgeball, players begin on different sides of a line and attempt to throw balls at players on the other side. However, in this no-loser version, if a player is hit with a ball she immediately runs to the other side (other team) and continues to play. Players are continuously throwing, dodging, hitting, being hit, and switching sides. The object is to end up with all players on one side, which requires a lot of hustling. You might also want to try having entire sides switch.

The game seems to work better with small teams. If there are five players on a side (which is ideal), we generally use four beach balls, four very soft rubber balls, or four pillows. With ten players per side we have eight or nine balls (or pillows) in play. The cross-over structure, together with the additional balls and a moderate-sized playing area, ensures that everyone is continuously involved. The game can also be played in pairs—for example, two on one pillow or towel tossing the ball or another pillow. Adjust the size of the playing area as needed.

Quieter, Inside Games

- *Aura.* Can human auras really draw people together? Here's a chance to find out. Partners stand facing each other and stretch their arms straight out in front until their palms are touching. Both partners then close their eyes, drop their hands, and turn in place three times. Keeping their eyes closed, they try to re-connect by touching the palms of either one of both hands. You can also play this game with three or more by forming a circle together.

- *Draw a Song.* The group is given a large sheet of paper and a Magic Marker. A player then chooses one of several slips of paper on which the leader has written the titles of well-known songs. She then brings this paper back to her group and, without speaking, draws clues to the particular song. The remaining children try to guess the song title from the creative clues. When someone guesses the right song, the entire group stands up, joins arms, and sings the song. A second person then chooses the title of another song.

  This game can also be adapted to draw clues to historical events, countries, famous people, and so on. It can also be played in pairs or trios, according to the size of the group.

- *Tweetie.* All eyes are closed. The leader whispers in one person's ear, "You're the tweetie." Keeping eyes closed, each person finds another's hand, shakes it, and asks, "Tweetie?" It sounds like a high-pitched little bird call. If both players ask "Tweetie?" the two drop hands and go on to someone else. The tweetie remains silent throughout the game. A player who gets no response to the question "Tweetie?" has found the tweetie and becomes part of it by holding on to the tweetie's hand and remaining silent from then on. Anyone shaking hands with any member of the tweetie becomes a part of it, and the tweetie grows larger and larger until everyone in the room is holding hands. Once the group has become one giant tweetie, the leader asks that all eyes open. If the players are having problems finding the tweetie, the size of the play space can be reduced or the bird can give out an unexpected chirp now and then.

- *Nonverbal Birthday Line-up.* The children are asked to try to line up according to the month and day of birth, "without any talking." Ready . . . go! This should inspire some interesting means of communication toward a common goal.

Partner Acrobatics

- *Human Supports.* Two people hold up a horizontal bar while another does a pull-up, a pull-over, or a knee-hang. The bar can be held at either chest height or shoulder height or over the head with arms straight. If necessary, four or five people can hold the bar up. Everyone takes a turn holding the bar and performing on the bar. The bar holders adjust or move the bar to help the performer.

- *Ladder Travel.* Another form of movement with human support. Players spread out along both sides of a sturdy ladder, bench, or plank, and lift it up so that it is held horizontally below their waists, with straight arms. One end of the ladder is lowered to the ground so that the "traveler" can step or crawl on it. The ladder is then slowly brought back up to a horizontal position, and the traveler walks or crawls across. Once he reaches the other end, this end is lowered so he can get off. The traveler then becomes a carrier for the next traveler. Depending upon the size and strength of the players, the ladder can be held horizontally at shoulder height or overhead (and perhaps even perpendicularly, with the right group and safety precautions). Ladder carriers can also walk around with the traveler sitting or crawling on the ladder, and/or rock the ladder back and forth.

Water Games

With proper supervision and normal water-safety precautions, water is a perfect medium for cooperative games, both in the natural outdoors and in a pool. Many of the games presented here can also be played in mud or snow.

- *Water Bridge.* The object of this game is to utilize all players to get one person across the shallow end of the pool without carrying him and without his going into the water. There is more than one way to do this. Here's an example: Players form two lines across the shallow end of the pool. The people in each line face one another and grasp wrists with the person across from them, forming a bridge. One person begins to crawl across the bridge but may run out of bridge unless the people forming the first part of the bridge run to the end as soon as the crawler has passed them.

For younger groups a story can be made up as to why the person (animal, princess, or whatever) must not get wet. For older groups the two lines of people can also try to pass a person overhead from one inner-tube island to another.

- *Log Chute.* Two lines are formed in the shallow end of the pool with the people in each line facing the other line and each joining hands with the person across from him. All players move their arms in a clockwise circular motion just below the surface of the water. As the water begins to move down the chute (area between two lines), the pair at the front of the line floats above the arms and down the current in the chute while lying on their backs, one after the other. They then move to the end of the chute, join hands, and keep the current moving for the next pair to chute.

- *Whirlpool.* Players form one large circle near one corner of the pool. The people in the circle join hands and move the circle around by walking as briskly as possible. As the water begins to ripple and the current begins to build up, people take turns breaking off and floating with the moving water away from the circle. The group can also form one large circle near the middle of the pool and, once the circle is moving fast, all let go at the same time and float outward on their backs with the current.

Collective-Score Games

The idea of two or more individuals or groups working together toward mutually beneficial ends is central to cooperative-game theory. Collective scoring is one means of allowing two or more teams to play toward a common end. One team does not achieve its success by competing *against* another or at the expense of another; rather, both "win" as a result of playing together.

As in the other cooperative games, flexibility is an important component. People with various skills and abilities can play. The number of players per side is adaptable. Players are free to change sides, as teams are no longer fixed and rigid or pitted against each other. Players can choose to serve the ball or play it from anywhere they wish. They can propel the ball with anything they want and in any manner they want. Balls of literally any size or shape can be used, including beach balls, pushballs (or monsterballs), regular balloons, or weather balloons. Any number of balls can be used. Standards (uprights to which nets are attached) can be 20 feet high or 2 inches high. Nets can be sloped, slooped, or even crisscrossed to form a large X, with one team in each of the four quadrants. The variations for collective play are limitless.

- *Togeth-air Ball (Collective-Score Volleyball).* An early version of this game was played by the Caribou Eskimo in the 1800s. The object was to keep a sealskin ball in motion without letting it touch the ground. No score was kept. In the contemporary version, one team is on each side of a line, rope, or net, and a ball is batted back and forth in a continuous fashion. It is a good idea to start this game with a balloon or beach ball before going on to something more difficult, like a volleyball. If a score is kept, it is a collective score. Children initially count one point any time *anyone* hits the ball, and see how many times they can hit the ball before it hits the ground. Team members from both sides can also chant out loud the number of consecutive hits.

Different rules may be applied for variations. The ball could be hit by different team members a certain number of times, or by all members ("all touch") before it goes over the net. "All touch" works best with sides of three or four each. Other variations include: unlimited hits per side, with points scored only when the ball goes over the net; two balls put into play at one time; players seeing how long a time they can keep the ball up rather than counting hits; players using the back of their hands, fists, elbows, heads, racquets, branches, air pumps, water shooters, plastic bats, Frisbees, fans, etc., to keep the ball up.

Another approach is to lower the net (or rope) so that a small rubber ball or tennis ball can be bounced back and forth. The object here is to hit the ball back and forth as many times as possible either on the bounce or on the fly. The open hand or a paddle-ball racquet can be used to propel the ball. Come up with your own variation.

- *Collective-Score Monsterball Volleyball.* This is a collective-score volleyball game using a gigantic hollow, canvas-covered rubber ball called a pushball, or monsterball. You can also use a weather balloon (see your local weatherman) or a bunch of beach balls in a large mesh sack or "potato sack," or you can order a pushball through your local sporting goods store. In this game players on each side of the net continuously bat or push the ball back and forth. Each time the ball goes over the net a collective point is scored. If the ball touches the floor, the counting begins over again. The large ball increases the number of people directly involved in getting it over the net, as one player usually cannot move the ball alone but needs help from teammates.

- *Bump and Scoot.* We rarely divide groups based on sex alone. However, in one school we found that the boys in grades 4 and 5 complained about playing with the girls, and when they did play together, the boys would hog the ball. In an attempt to solve this problem, we came up with the following game. Boys started on one side of a net and girls on the other. Whenever a person on one team hit the beach ball over the net, she (or he) scooted under the net to the other side. Rather than a collective score, the common objective was to make a complete change in teams with as few drops of the ball as possible.

When we played this, an interesting thing occurred. Boys started to "feed" girls, teams became happily integrated, and everyone played together in order to help all team members exchange sides. To complete the exchange, it is best to have several games going at once in different parts of the gym, so that there are not too many on each team. Bump and Scoot can also be played for a collective score only, where all players merely attempt to keep the ball or balls going back and forth as many times as possible.

- *Bump and Team Scoot.* This outgrowth of Bump and Scoot provides for a little more action, particularly with larger teams. The object is to score as many consecutive collective Bump and Team Scoots as possible. Four teams are formed. Teams 1 and 2 start on one side of the net, and Teams 3 and 4 start on the other side. Each team chooses a code name. When a player hits the ball over the net, she yells her team's code name, and her whole team scoots under the net. It will keep them scooting, especially if you use two balls. For another variation, have only team members who have touched or helped set the ball up scoot under the net when the ball is bumped over.

- *Collective Blanketball.* Two teams of about eight or ten each spread out around two sturdy blankets or similar-sized pieces of durable material. They grasp the edges of the blanket, and a beach ball or monsterball is placed in the middle of one. To warm up, groups toss the ball into the air and catch it again in the blanket or roll the ball around the outside edges of the blanket. Teams then pass one ball back and forth by tossing it in unison toward the receiving team. One team can also toss their ball straight up and dash out of the way to let the other team dash under it to catch it with their blanket.

You can also give each team its own ball, so that they can exchange them by simultaneously tossing their ball toward the other team on a signal that is already agreed upon.

For groups seeking additional challenge, juggling can be attempted by trying to get two or more balls going in the air in a continuous manner. This can be attempted initially by one team alone, making sure one of two balls is always in the air, and later by tossing balls from team to team. To involve more people use a sturdy bedspread, a large piece of lightweight canvas, or a parachute. A variation of this game, known as Collective Netting, can be played in shallow water with a fishnet instead of a blanket.

- *Collective-Score Blanketball.* Two teams use a blanket to toss a beach ball (or a large pushball) back and forth over a volleyball net. Every time the ball is tossed over the net by one team and caught successfully in the blanket held by the other team, one collective point is scored. This game is extremely cooperative in structure, as every team member is a part of every toss and every catch made by his or her team. In addition, both teams work together toward a common end. There remains the collective challenge of scoring as many points in a row as possible.

This game has been very well received by a variety of age groups. We once had three different Collective-Score Blanketball games going all at once, taking up the whole length of a large gym. At one point I looked up from behind a monsterball and saw another monsterball being tossed sideways to an adjoining team on the same side of the gym. Another group had two beach balls going through the air at the same time. Players were having fun experimenting with different-sized balls, blankets, and even towels.

- *Balloon Bucket (Collective Hoops).* One balloon or beach ball is provided for every two children. For a group of twenty, about eight or ten hula hoops are spread out on the floor around the edges of the playing area. Partners bat the balloons back and forth in a nonstop fashion as they attempt to score. In order to score, one of the partners must manage to pick up a hoop, get the balloon to pass through it, replace the hoop on the floor, and continue on with her partner to the next hoop while still batting the balloon back and forth. The object of the game is for the entire group to score collectively as many hoops as possible in a certain time period (for example, five minutes for twenty people). No player can run while holding the balloon. No player can bat the balloon twice in succession. It must be hit by one partner and then the other.

This is a totally active game with total involvement and a great deal of cooperation. It can be played with groups of any size merely by adjusting the number of hoops that are put out. It can also be played in teams of three rather in pairs.

- *Collective Orbit.* This is our cooperative adaptation of a more competitively structured game called Orbit. In Collective Orbit, one group of players forms one large circle and another group of players forms a smaller circle inside the other. The inside players lie down on their backs (on mats, grass, or sand) with their heads pointing toward the center point of the circle and their feet propped up in a bicycling position. The outside players stand with arms ready for action. The objective of the game is for all the players to work together to keep a monsterball in play while moving it around the circle. The ball alternates between the inside players, who kick it with their feet to the outside players, and the outside players, who push it back in with their hands. An attempt is made by both teams to keep the ball from touching the ground. The number of times the ball is exchanged between inside and outside circles can be counted aloud. For additional action a beach ball can be passed around the outside circle (using hands) while the monsterball is in play.

- *Collective Volley Orbit.* This is a combination of Collective Orbit and Collective-Score Monsterball. One orbit group (an inner semicircle of people on their backs with their feet facing the net, propped up for action, and an outer circle of people on their feet with hands propped for action) is stationed on each side of a net. The people on the inside semicircle attempt to kick the ball over the net, and the people in the outer circle try to receive the ball and bump it to the inside semicircle so they can put it into orbit. (Everyone works together to prevent the ball from touching the floor.) Each time the ball goes over the net and is caught (lands safely) on the other side, one collective orbit is achieved. If the ball hits the floor, it is a crash landing, and it must be "relaunched." The size of the ball and the height of the net can be adjusted to suit the group, and players can rotate between inside and outside circles.

One variation is to have the people in the outside circles pair off using towels to receive the ball and to set up the inside semicircle for their blast into orbit.

- *All on One Side.* Did you ever hear of a volleyball game that starts with a team of four or five players on one side of the net and no team on the other side? Well, now you have. The object is to get your team to the other side of the net and back as many times as possible. Using a balloon for a ball, each player volleys the balloon to another player and then scoots under the net to the other side. The last player to touch the balloon taps it over the net and scoots under. The receiving players try to keep the balloon in play and repeat the process. As the team gets better, try putting two balloons into play at one time.

- *Collective Stone.* This no-loser game combines total involvement in batting, fielding, and scoring. Four or five bases are spread out on the field or floor. One person starts at home plate and propels an object into the field of play by batting, kicking, shooting, or throwing it. She then proceeds to round the bases as quickly as possible. She must circle completely around each base (rather than touching it) before proceeding on to the next base. The fielders retrieve the object (ball, puck, bean bag, Frisbee, water balloon, pumpkin) and pass it around to all fielders. When the last person in the field receives the object, he yells, "Stone!" The person who propelled it must then stop stone-cold in her tracks, no matter where she is, even if she is between two bases. Another fielder then goes up to home plate, propels the object, and starts to round the bases. Any "stoned" runners in the field can continue on their circuit once the object is propelled into the field of play by the next batter. Each batter tries to get as far around the bases as possible before someone yells, "Stone!" A point is scored every time a person completes the full circuit around the bases. The game continues until the collective score equals the number of players, which should mean that every player has scored one point.

This game can be played as a modified version of hockey (shooting puck), kickball, inner-tube water polo (throwing ball from tube), softball, football (throwing ball into field), broomball, scooterball, or whatever the players decide. The number of marker bases and the distance they are spread apart will depend upon the game being played, the players' skill level, and the number of participants. Adjustments can be made once the game has started so that the time to complete the circuit with a well-placed ball and the time for fielders to pass the ball to everyone are very close. Fielders can also use different methods to pass the ball to one another. They can all run toward the ball and quickly pass it to one another; they can stay in their position on the field, letting the closest person trap the ball and then pass it around; they can all run toward the ball, form a line, and pass the ball from person to person under their legs, and so on.

• *Deacove Rounders.* This is a beautiful example of how one person (Jim Deacove) turned a sport like baseball into a new children's game of helping. As in competitive baseball, there are two teams. Here, however, each team stays up at bat until it scores the number of runs equal to the number of players on the team. If there are five players on a team, it must get five runs to fill the quota. If a grounder is hit, the batter advances one base; on an infield fly, two bases; on an outfield fly, three bases. When runners are on base, they are bumped up or move ahead as their teammates get hits.

Now here's the clincher! The team in the field must stop the ball before a hit counts. On a grounder, the ball must be fielded before it stops; for a fly, the ball must be caught to count. Remember, though, the fielders are trying to get the ball not to put the other team out but to ensure that the batter gets on base. For one team to fill its quota, it needs the help of the other team. For the fielding team to get up to bat, they have to help the batting team fill its quota. Batters generally get three pitches and rotate back into the order if they don't get a hit; but the pitcher has a reason to provide good ones. Fielders rotate through the different positions during the course of the game.

This game can also be played as a modified version of teeball, where the ball is placed on a chest-high, stationary, upright tee (semiflexible plastic pipe works well as an upright). The batter swings until he or she bats the ball (tees off) into play.

- *Reverse Score.* If you want a game that really plays with the contemporary concept of winning and losing, try a reverse-score game. Every time you score on the other team, they get a point. It's a gift! If you want to add further to the confusion, have no goalies and have the players who score switch to the "winning" team, which is the team with the most points, but actually the weakest team, because it got its points by being scored upon. When it's all over, try asking who won!

- *Incrediball.* A great cooperative game still waiting to be invented. See what you can come up with!

The More We Get Together

the little people's games: cooperative play with preschoolers

When we first started to play with preschool children, I remember being concerned about how to get a group of little kids together in one spot, let alone get them to cooperate in a game. But we persisted, we adapted, we racked our brains and scaled down our games. As a result some very interesting and gratifying things emerged over the course of a year. Not only did the children begin to cooperate within the games, but acts of togetherness began to fill their unstructured play outside the games as well.

We discovered two basic "problems" when working with three- and four-year-old children. First, we did not have the games (or instructions) broken down into simple enough steps. This usually became obvious within a few minutes: the children didn't know what to do or the game simply did not work. Often you can adapt things right on the spot by immediately breaking larger ideas down into little steps, guiding the kids through the action, or scaling down the challenge. It helps if you join in play with the children, at least until they are familiar with

Big Turtle

the game. Sometimes, despite all efforts, a game may really bomb out, and you just have to chalk it up to experience and think about how you can alter the situation for the next game session.

A personally more disconcerting problem we faced was the fact that one or two children in a couple of groups chose not to join in the cooperative play. These children who do not join in are usually the ones who could benefit most from the experience. They often do not have appropriate skills for interacting with others in a positive way or do not feel accepted. Keith, a little lad of four, sat on the sidelines the moment he entered the gym. The teacher informed me that he was not that well coordinated and was probably "afraid to join in" a game. A mere four years in this world and already acutely aware that games are for the skilled! What do I do in such situations?

First I try to encourage them to join in. "Come on, Keith, these are real fun games, you'll like them" kind of thing. If that doesn't work, I try sending other kids over to get them, especially if a game requires two or three players. Next I ask them to be my partner. That sometimes works, sometimes not.

As I continue to meet with these "I don't wanna play" setbacks, there is one thing I feel I have going for me: I make sure that the kids always come into the gym, even if they do not want to play any games. At least I know that are watching the other kids play. Perhaps they will see that it's fun, that everyone is accepted, and that they don't have to be that good. They also learn how the game works and how the children play together as a unit to make it work. I wait and watch and encourage and wait some more. They wait and watch and wait some more. In the end, they will usually get involved. After eight weeks, for instance, Keith joined in his first game on his own accord. I breathed a sigh of relief.

What is crystal-clear from such experiences is that you have to take your time with children. Things don't always happen instantaneously. You must fight your own disappointment when change does not occur overnight. It takes time to learn to be cooperative and considerate, particularly when other social forces are pulling in another direction. It takes time to develop feelings of trust and acceptance, more time for some kids than others.

Most preschool and kindergarten teachers are already aware of this fact. One teacher who tried some of my co-op games with four-year-olds wrote me a letter saying:

> The children have just begun to help put away equipment. I started with pushing benches back to the wall. At first they were on both sides so the bench went in circles. Then one child said, "Everyone on one side and push." It took about 2–3 minutes to get it there (and a bench dropped on a foot—nothing serious) but they cheered when they finished. They also now put their own little mats away and are quite good at cooperating.

A few of the co-op games she introduced to the children were initially met with "disaster," but patience and persistence eventually led to success.

Just as games must be designed with the child in mind, so must play equipment be designed or adapted specifically for young children. We desperately need play materials that make it easy for little people to cooperate and likely for them to succeed. We should design at least some playground and playroom equipment that functions well only when two or more children play together to make it work (e.g., tricycles built for two, swings built for three, rocking horses built for four, roly-polies, balancing boards, and slides built for five or six, and so on). Children can be encouraged to construct their own equipment together, to move it into place together, and to play with it together. They can move with it, within it, under it, on top of it, or through it, or make it move together. We could benefit from more cooperative play "props," such as giant potato sacks or giant cater-

Caterpillar Over the Mountain

Cooperative Musical Hoops

Cooperative Musical Chairs

Numbers, Shapes, and Letters Together

pillar covers, which allow more than one child to play together at the same time. We also need balls, bats, boats, nets, pucks, fields, standards, and playground and gymnastic equipment designed with little people's success in mind.

Dads, there's one point I'd like to mention which too many of you overlook: *both* parents can participate in preschool activities with their kids. At least in the cooperative nursery schools and kindergartens in which I've worked, I've seen only mothers taking the time to volunteer as assistant teachers on a regular rotational basis.

I'd like to to tell you, dads, that you're missing out on a novel experience. Watching three-, four-, and five-year-olds come up with their own innovative interpretations of games gives a pleasure hard to describe. Even if your excuses are good, what you ought to realize is not only that you are denying your child a few moments of important camaraderie, but also that you are denying yourself a chance to participate in his or her one brief childhood. Just remember, the time you spend playing and listening—and learning—is all part of a larger process of caring for and about your child.

Outside of the classroom or playschool, a fine occasion to put some of these new cooperative games into play can be children's birthday parties. These are, after all, intended to be celebrations, and not places for fighting and crying—as is too often the case when children play traditional party games that create losers.

One inventive mother took the occasion of her five-year-old son's birthday to adapt the traditional favorite Pin the Tail on the Donkey in a new cooperative way. In her version, children helped each other pin the tail on the donkey by calling directions out to the blindfolded person. In another adaptation, they worked together to assemble the entire animal on the wall, each taking turns adding a different body part—leg, head, tail— and again directing the blindfolded person to the proper place on the wall. The results were lots of cheers and absolutely no tears.

An article on my little people's games inspired another mom to invent a new version of Hide and Seek. In her Cooperative Hide and Seek, two children (hand in hand) began as seekers while the rest of the children hid around the house. Each time they found someone they took him or her by the hand and together the group would seek another "hider." It apparently "took a lot of cooperation to get everyone going in the same direction," but the results were worth the effort. For Cooperative Hide and Seek it is also possible to have a whole group seeking together one child who is "lost in the bush" (even if the bush happens to be behind or under the couch).

Little people can also show each other how to use, move, or make equipment and can likewise teach each other games or parts of games. One means of children's cooperative-games teaching resembles a jigsaw puzzle with each child contributing one piece of the puzzle. If a game has three simple rules, each of three children is given one rule of the game, which is pictured on a card. The children get together in a little group and each explains his specific rule so that all three children can then play the game.

Cooperative Musical Chairs

remaking adult games

Many of the games nobody loses previously discussed, particularly the collective-score games, can be played successfully and enjoyably by teen-agers and adults, as long as the game is kept appropriately challenging for the group. For many they will become "the best games in town." Some people, though, may still prefer games that are more traditionally competitive in structure. The focus of this section will be on keeping the fun and involvement in these games. Our objective then becomes happy, healthy, fun-filled, cooperative competition (i.e., semicooperative games). We still want everyone leaving the game to feel somehow enriched by the experience. It is possible for this to happen, even within competitive structures, but only if the right conditions and spirit are kept in the game. In the end it is one's perception of winning or losing, and particularly one's perception of the importance of score-board winning or losing, that is the important thing—not the "win" or "loss"

itself. The game experience itself, and not any numerical score, will help us think about and remake the many ways of winning.

Peter Hopkins from the University of Waterloo has successfully put some "semicooperative" principles into practice in an innovative university intramural program where:

1. There are no officials. Self-control and peer control regulate the game.

2. There are only minimal rules, which are flexible and are agreed upon at the beginning of the game or adjusted during the game.

3. There are no extrinsic awards (trophies, crests, and so on).

4. No standings or league statistics are kept.

5. Keeping score is optional.

6. Teams can have any number on a side as long as they have equal numbers.

7. There is no set of rules for eligibility. Anyone can participate.

8. There is free substitution in every activity. When tired you just run off the floor and someone else runs on.

9. There are minimal stoppages in play because there are no officials.

10. The games by their nature and lack of rigid rules reduce the emphasis on comparing people's skill levels.

How are these principles transformed into action? In floor hockey or ball hockey, all walls are in play and there are no officials, no offsides, and no face-offs. Consequently there is very little stoppage in play. There is one hour slotted for each game. Within this time period the captains, together with their teams, determine the start and end of the game as well as the length of half-time. If desired, all the available time can be spent playing.

For instance, in coed slow-pitch softball, you pitch slowly *to your own team* with unlimited pitches in which to hit the ball. Every batter hits every inning. In volleyball, rules like carrying the ball, touching the net, hitting the ball twice in a row, are not worried about. In seven-on-a-side touch football, there are forward passes allowed from any point, at any time, and every player is an eligible receiver. In inner-tube water polo, swimming ability is not a criterion for play, since everyone sits in inner tubes. With the emphasis on fun and activity rather than on winning, the intensity of the games is reduced, resulting in less aggression, more participation, and more fun for the participants. Hopkins's "fun program" has met with overwhelming success and now includes over 168 teams—more, I might add, than the competitive intramural program at the same university.

It's interesting to see what happens once people are provided with a choice. In speaking about his program, Hopkins said, "If one team doesn't have enough

Collective Blanketball

players, the other team will share. If you want to play with seven to a side in volleyball, then play with seven. There's no reason for people having to stand on the sidelines. Nobody worries about gaining a play-off spot because there are no play-offs. Nobody cares about getting two points if you win a game." Perhaps the most gratifying thing of all is "actually to see adults having fun. Watching them laughing and joking while playing is like night and day compared to competitive sports." For more complete details of Hopkins's playful program, see the Appendix.

Ian McGregor, director of recreation at British Columbia's, Simon Fraser University, introduced an innovative Alternate Program in intramurals for the first time in the fall of 1977. The program features no registration, no officiating, no scores, no standings, no set teams, and no commitment to continue—unless you enjoy yourself. The only structured part of the program is that the gym, some equipment, and an assistant (who will provide instruction, if desired) are made available at specific times. Alternate Activities include Rotational Volleyball, where the server rotates to the other team, along with basketball, floor hockey, and soccer, where players rotate between teams.

Bill Harper and his coworkers have also come up with some interesting alternatives at their Kansas State College "play factory," which was responsible for university-wide play. Among other things they have eliminated officials, rigid schedules, and boundary lines. They tried soccer, softball, and touch football without lines, and found that they were more playful games than the "play-in-a-box" versions. They have also played on stilts, on airplane tire tubes, and in mud holes, and have even held a tobacco-spit contest. They are now experimenting with new sports such as the 50-yard crawl, the shot roll, the 120-yard underhurdle, the low jump (a clean leap under a bar that would be lowered after each jump), an underwater jacks tournament, basketball with moving baskets, an all-day handhold.

Lou Fabian and Kathy Evans from the University of Pittsburgh have introduced a new form of Recreational Basketball based upon cooperative principles. It was clear to them that the competitive intramural program "did not meet the needs of all the people." Consequently they attempted to develop a noncompetitive alternative that would give individuals a choice. In 1977, for the first time, all teams registering in their intramural basketball program were presented with a collective-score option. Total score for both teams represented winners in the recreation league. In addition, players called their own fouls and turnovers. There was free substitution on the run (with no stoppage in play), no foul shooting or jump balls, and no team standings were kept.

In their first year, twenty teams (ten women's teams and ten men's teams) opted to play Recreational Collective-Score Basketball. Firsthand observation and feedback from these participants indicated a successful beginning, a participatory situation that "operates at a faster pace, thus providing more physical exercise, promotes cooperation of both teams toward a mutual goal, fosters development of positive social interaction, and provides an environment where ability is not a prime consideration for who does or does not play." The future for them is right now, putting their ideas to the test in the real world. As they said, "We will not know unless we try . . . and that's the bottom line."

In addition to playing down the importance of scoreboard winning, various strategies can be employed within different types of game structures to bring everyone into the action, to equalize teams, to rotate positions, to provide for success experiences, and to gain some element of cooperation. If you closely observe a game such as indoor soccer, you will discover that some players never even touch the ball. How can they feel involved? One cooperative strategy to alleviate this problem is called "All Touch." Before a shot is taken, the ball must be passed to and touched by all members of your team. A similar strategy can be implemented in scoring. In All Score or Four Score, either all the players or four different players must make a goal before a team can win. Before long, players begin to include all players in the action spontaneously even when such "rules" are no longer in effect. We usually use oversized goals for additional fun when playing All Score in sports such as soccer.

A high school basketball coach enrolled in one of my courses suggested a scoring modification in order to increase cooperation among team members and to avoid situations where one player scores most (or all) of the points. The idea was to subtract the difference between the high and low scorers' point totals from their team's total score. For example, let's assume one team scored 30 points, with their high scorer netting 10 points and their low scorer getting 0 points. The team's final score would be 20 (30 minus 10, or the total score minus the difference between high and low scorers). If another team scored 24 points, with the high scorer getting 6 points and the low scorer getting 2, their final score would also be 20 points (24 minus 4). You could also give bonus points to a team for every member that scored (e.g., 2 bonus points awarded for every player who scores), or 10 bonus points only if all team members score, or double the number of points of the lowest scorer on the team as a bonus. This certainly gives coaches a good

Big People's Big Sack

reason to play everybody and encourages the development of new and exciting game tactics.

Rotational strategies can be introduced, either within one team or between two teams. For *within-team rotation* the players simply rotate through the various positions during the course of the game, so that everyone gets to play every position. Players are no longer subjected to rigid decisions like "you play outfield," "you play goalie," "you block," for the rest of their "playing" lives. The rules don't allow it. For *between-team rotation*, the rotational process extends to the other team. It can be done in virtually any sport. In Rotational Volleyball, for example, the rotation of players follows through both teams. (This tends to allow players to focus on the process, on the "here and now.") How can you get mad at the other team or lose to the other team when you are or will become the other team at some point in time?

Some people prefer to reserve the between-team trades or rotation of players for situations where teams are obviously not balanced in terms of ability. Lopsided scores don't usually provide the best kind of challenge for anyone. It's better to give the other team an extra player or two, or to switch a few players during the course of the game, to even things up. The ultimate objective here is to have teams so evenly matched that they play to a tie. Uneven teams can also be evened up without making player exchanges. One way of doing this is to make adjustments in the size of the goal. For example, larger buckets or more buckets could be placed at one end of the court (for modified basketball), or a long bench could serve as the goal at one end of the field and a short one at the other for soccer.

Bucketball is a form of basketball with moving baskets. Team members attempt to score on their own goalie at the other end of the court, who has a wastepaper basket (bucket) in his hands. The goalie stands on a chair or slightly raised platform and helps his teammates to score by moving the bucket in the direction of the shot.

Another strategy involves the rotation of players during the course of a tournament rather than during the course of a game. This was done in a provincial hockey-league tournament for house-league players in Victoria, British Columbia. The composition of each team constantly changed during the tournament. Winning was de-emphasized. Social interaction and making new friends became the focal points.

John Salmela from the University of Montreal hosted a citywide rotational gymnastics meet with a slightly different tack. Gymnasts from different schools and clubs were placed on teams based upon their coaches' assessments of their ability, in order to have relatively equal teams. Former competitors helped and

"Two at Once" Collective Blanketball

cheered their new-found teammates. New bonds were formed, particularly between very young gymnasts and their older counterparts.

Larry Vea of Glenayre School in Port Moody, British Columbia, successfully applied similar principles in an upper elementary school interschool sports program. All students interested in participating were placed on a team, with an attempt being made to equalize teams within each school. Friendships were often built between schools by having half of a team's members originate from one school and half originate from another. Other definite pluses of the program included the fact that no players were "cut," everybody was given equal playing time during games, teams were kept small to ensure adequate playing time for each person, and no compilation of records or scores were kept. Because the scoreboard "stakes" weren't so high and because teams were mixed, a relaxed and healthy atmosphere permeated most games.

I'd love to see this kind of thing done on an international level in sports to really bring countries together, to move beyond competition for cooperation and mutual understanding. An alternative structure for Olympic competition (or noncompetition) might include volleyball teams or swimming relay teams, comprising of members from several countries. When national teams tour other countries, why not have teams made up of members from both sides?

cooperative games
from other cultures

The more I study other cultures and their play, the more I realize how restrictive is our contemporary view of play and games. Clearly ours is not the world view. I am presenting the following examples of cooperative games from other cultures in hopes of broadening your horizons of game forms. Let your thoughts wander. Reflect upon the concepts behind the games. Str-e-e-e-tch your mind. Maybe you can come up with your own adaptation of some of these games to play in your own gym or playground; you might like to use the North American Indians' method for choosing sides, for example. But the most important thing is to think about the lessons you can draw from these games, for that is why I have chosen to share them with you.

Aboriginal Games

- *Aboriginal Infinity Marbles*. This marble game played by Australian Aboriginal children has an interesting no-loser twist. Two players sit facing each other, cross-legged, about 10 feet apart. Each player has a small cluster of marbles on the ground directly in front of him. The players take turns attempting to hit the other person's marbles by rolling one of their own marbles. An astute observer described the game in the following way: "When a 'shot' was successful, the hit marbles were delivered to the successful shooter, who placed them with his others. [If not successful, the marble remains where it stopped.] As a result this game could go on *ad infinitum*, as one cluster diminished in size and consequently became harder to hit while the other cluster became easier because of its increased size."

Another version of marbles without losers was played almost daily in the summer months by Eskimo children living on the Bering coast of Alaska. Each child brought one marble to the game, played with it, and left with the same marble. The game had no provisions for winning another player's marble. There was simply no need to walk off with another child's marble in order to have either challenge or fun. Small groups of children merely came together to enjoy themselves and to enjoy the challenge of hitting the scattered marbles. In fact, the "winning" version of marbles, which we are accustomed to, detracted from the fun and the children chose not to play it.

• *Pin.* This game of cooperation is played by Indian children in Guatemala. A wooden pin is set up at a moderate distance from a throwing line. (The group can decide the length.) The object is for the team to work together to get the first ball that is rolled (lead ball) to touch the pin without knocking the pin over. The first player rolls his ball and the subsequent team members try to roll their balls so that they nudge the lead ball closer to the pin. The game is won when the lead ball is touching the pin. If the pin is knocked over, the player who knocked it over starts a new game by rolling the first ball.

• *Choosing Sides.* In many of the games played by technologically "primitive" people, sides (where they existed) seemed to develop spontaneously and change readily. As more structured games were introduced, North American Indians came up with two interesting procedures for choosing sides which ensured that no players were excluded or humiliated by being chosen last. In one method the chief sat inside a circle at the center of the field. All the players' sticks (e.g., for lacrosse) were placed in a heap in front of him. After being blindfolded, he picked sticks two at a time and placed one on his right and one on his left until all sticks were gone. Players then ran to the two piles of sticks, found their own, and joined that team. Another method of choosing teams was for the chief to place strips of two different colors of paper in a small pouch or covered basket. Each player drew one slip of paper and was designated to a team by the color chosen.

Cooperative Games from New Guinea

The following noncompetitive games have been observed being played by the peaceful and cooperative Motu and Tangu people of New Guinea.

- *Manumanu (Little Bird).* One child stands on a long wooden plank, which is raised off the ground and carried to and fro by her peers. While holding a stick as a balancing rod, she sings and dances on the moving plank. The children take turns being the little bird and helping keep the *manumanu* in flight.

- *Evanena (Looking Down the Pole).* Two rows of children face each other and make a platform of linked arms. One boy stands up on the arms of the last two in line and walks forward across the joined arms of the others. As he moves along the platform, the boys he passes run to the front of the line, continuing to extend the platform even as the walker progresses. The game thus goes on until the walker finally falls off.

- *Kabele (Hit It).* One boy throws a coconut and another tries to spear it in flight. The children take turns throwing and spearing.

In many of the group games of the Motu people that are described as "noncompetitive," when one group achieves its goal it merely changes places with the other group and gives the other group a chance to achieve its goal. For example, in Parpoparo (Little Fish), two circles are formed in the water, one inside the other. Members of the inner circle try to pass through the outer circle by swimming underwater. While singing and beating on the water, members of the outer circle use their bodies to block the passage. If any member of the inner circle swims through the outer circle, the circles reverse roles, and so the game continues.

- *Taketak.* Taketak is a popular game played by the Tangu people of New Guinea, in which the objective is to tie, not to win (in our sense of winning). The game represents the dominant theme in Tangu culture, that of moral equality. The name Taketak comes from the Tangu word for the hard spines of coconut fronds or leaves. To play the game, these spines (or *taketaks*) are stripped of their leaves and struck into the ground in two separate lots. Each lot contains about thirty taketaks and is separated from the other lot by about five yards. The taketaks themselves are staked about 6 inches apart and in a manner which ensures that they do not form parallel or diagonal lines, which would allow tops to

Taketak

be thrown down empty corridors. Hollow homemade tops, 2 or 3 inches in diameter, which are thrown at the taketaks, are made by forcing a spindle through the center of a dried jungle fruit.

Two teams are formed, each of which have the same number of tops and approximately the same number of players. To start the game, one player spins his top in the palm of his hand and, in one motion, throws it into one of the lots of taketaks, trying to hit as many as possible. Any taketaks which are touched while the top is either in flight or spinning on the ground are pulled out and laid aside. Once all the players from both teams have thrown their tops into their respective lots, Round 1 is over. Unless the score is equal at that point, one of the two teams replaces a couple of taketaks in their lot, and both teams go through a second round in the same manner as the first.

Let's suppose the first team struck three taketaks (and therefore removed three taketaks) in the first round, and the second team struck (and removed) two. The first team replaces two taketaks into their lot. Now Team 1 has one taketak removed and Team 2 has two removed. If, on their second round, the first team hits one taketak, it is removed, leaving both teams with two taketaks out of their lots. Both teams are now equivalent as to the number of taketaks removed, but the second team still has to have their second round of throwing. Their object is now to throw their tops into their lot without hitting any taketaks. If their tops are thrown fairly into the middle of their lot, and they succeed in not hitting any, the game is won and both teams are declared equivalent. If on the other hand the second team should hit one taketak, they have now removed three and are not yet equivalent. Since the round is over and the score is not tied, Team 2 replaces two taketaks. The game continues in this manner until a draw is reached or until the players tire, agree that they are equal, and suspend the game. Tying requires the refined skill (and good fortune) of being able to hit taketaks when necessary and miss them when expedient.

A game designed to end in a tie is intriguing in itself and opens up many new possibilities. Continual replacement (in this case, of taketaks) is also an important concept that allows the game to continue until an equal score is reached or until there is mutual agreement that it is time to stop. Replacement may occur in several ways. Perhaps the simplest way is for the teams to take turns replacing two taketaks after each round of play. Another possibility, which serves to keep teams and scores relatively equal, is for the team which has the most taketaks removed after each round of play to replace two taketaks. Still another possibility is for the team which has the most taketaks removed after each round to replace the total number of taketaks that the other team has removed. For example, Team 1 has seven out and Team 2 has three; Team 1 therefore replaces three taketaks into their lot. Lastly, we could consider the possibility of having the higher scoring team replace the number of taketaks that represents the difference between the two teams. For example, Team 1 has seven out and Team 2 has three; Team 1 therefore replaces four taketaks, and another full round begins. There are all kinds of potentials to be explored which relate to replacement and equivalence.

This concept of playing to a tie is not restricted to the Tangu people. The Asmat of New Guinea used to race dug-out canoes across a river but always reached the other side at the same instant. When soccer was first introduced to their children, they played to a tie. When Eskimo youth began cross-country skiing, they skied hard but tried to cross the finish line at the same instant, and Australian Aboriginal children often ran races to a tie. I tried this one day when I was out running with a friend. It was kind of fun because you're never quite sure of the other's strategy. You run hard and they run hard, they slow down and you slow down. The last 40 or 50 yards, when you are usually clipping along at a healthy pace, is all anticipation. How are we going to hit the line at the same instant? Then . . . victory!

Nuglutang

Inuit (Eskimo) Games
from the Canadian Arctic

● *Nuglutang.* This used to be a very popular game of sharing played particularly during the months of darkness. In it a spindle-shaped piece of caribou antler with a hole drilled through it is hung above the players' heads so that it dangles at about shoulder height. The players stand around the target holding sharp rods, something like shortened pencils but made out of bone. Each person then tries to push the tip of his rod into the hole in the target, all at the same time. This sets the target swinging all over the place. The first person to place his rod in the target is the "winner" and puts up as a stake anything he wishes that has value, such as a harpoon head or knife, and retires from the play. The second winner assumes ownership of the first stake, but in turn replaces it with another. The game continues this way until the lone last player manages to nail the target. As the game is then finished, he does not have to replace the stake. Thus the only person to "lose" anything (in our terms) was the first "winner," and the only one to win anything was the last "winner" (loser?). This game was played amid peals of laughter, and many excess goods were exchanged.

- *Blanket Toss.* Originally a large durable blanket was made by sewing together several walrus hides. The blanket was about 10 to 12 feet wide. One player would sit or stand in the middle of the blanket, and a group of twenty or thirty players would spread out around the blanket and catapult the middle person high into the air. The blankets used today are large circular canvas structures with a heavy rope intertwined around the edge for a secure grip. This forms something like a very large circular trampoline, propelled by the power of the people co-operating around the edge.

- *Muk (Silence).* This game centers around laughter. Players begin by sitting in a circle. One player moves into the middle of the circle. He then chooses another player, who must say "Muk" and then remain silent and straight-faced. The person in the middle uses comical expressions and gestures to try to "break the muk." The player to break the muk is dubbed with a comical name and replaces the person in the middle.

- *Kaipsak (Spinning Tops).* This was a favorite among Inuit children. Each child, in turn, would spin his top and then race outside the icehouse, run around it, and try to get back in before the top stopped spinning. In the wintertime children would become the tops themselves by sitting on a block of ice and being spun around by the other children until they became too dizzy to stay in the seat. The next "rider" would then take a turn. The children would occasionally hook up one of their dogs to a block of ice and have a whirl. Lots of fun.

- *Eagle Carry.* In what used to be called the Spread Eagle Carry, now referred to as the Airplane Carry, one person lays face-down with arms stretched out straight. Three carriers pick him up, two by the wrists and one by the ankles, and carry him as far as possible before he collapses. The eagle is carried slowly, usually about a foot or two off the ground, and lowered gently as he begins to collapse. In this game, all of the birds smile before taking off, and most of them smile after landing. Crash landings can sometimes retard bird smiles but do not seem to inhibit laughter from the rest of the flock.

- *Dog Sledge.* When speaking of Inuit children, Samuel King Hutton, an early explorer, wrote,

For sheer merriment there is nothing to beat the sledge game without dogs, when six or seven of the boys slip the harness on their own shoulders and race away with the sledge, wheeling this way and that at the command of their driver. They enter most heartily into the fun, crossing from one place to another in the team, just as dogs do, snapping and yelping and whining and tugging to be on the move every time the driver calls a halt.

A similar kind of game can be played with toboggans, on modern snow sleds, or on a floating mattress in shallow water. A variation that can be played in a gym involves the use of a dolly or a four-wheeled scooter and a thick rope. One child (the driver) sits, kneels, or stands on the sledge (dolly), and three or four others grasp the rope, thereby becoming sledge dogs. To slow the game down to a walk or safe trot, the dogs' vision can be impaired by flopping a large brown paper bag over their heads. They can see down (and perhaps to the side) but not straight ahead. The driver directs the dogs through the course (around a series of marker cones). For younger children this same concept can be tied into Christmas activities with Santa and his reindeer.

Eagle Carry

Chinese Nursery School Games

These games were viewed in the People's Republic of China during a visit to a nursery school/kindergarten.

- *Helping Harvest the Land.* Teams are made up of six members; each team needs a hoe, some cardboard flowers, a watering can, a manure bucket, a spray can, a basket, and a tricycle. The equipment is placed at the far end of the yard, and the teams line up at the near end. The first person in each team runs down to his team's equipment, picks up the hoe, and hoes the ground (about five strokes), then runs back. The second person plants the cardboard (or plastic) flowers and runs back. The third is responsible for watering the flowers. The fourth spreads the fertilizer. The fifth sprays the flowers to protect them. The sixth person harvests the flowers, puts them in the basket, hops on the tricycle, and rides back, taking the flowers to market.

- *Big Turnip.* This is another harvesting game in which one child pretends he is a big turnip growing in the ground. A single child cannot pull him out of the ground ("pick him"), because the turnip is too large. A pre-determined number of pullers are needed before the turnip can be pulled out of the ground. The objective is for children to learn that you can accomplish working together what you cannot accomplish alone.

- *So-Fa Game.* Half the children form a circle and begin to sing a song and clap their hands. The other half of the children skip around inside the circle clapping their hands. On a specific word in the song the children inside the circle stop in front of someone in the outer circle and play a quick pat-a-cake routine. They then clap their hands together, spin around quickly, shake hands with the person in front of them, and change places.

creating
your own games;
evaluating your success

It is through the creation and sharing of positive alternatives that we will ultimately come up with our most enjoyable and impactful games. But just inventing new games is not enough, because they can still reflect highly competitive or destructive orientations. It is the framework or structure of the game that is so vitally important. What kind of response does the game demand—competitive or cooperative, hurtful or helpful? Will anyone be left out? Will everyone be fully involved in the action? Will there be a sense of losing? Will everyone leave happier than when they began? Is the game designed or structured in a way that will hurt anyone psychologically or physically?

People (particularly adults) often tend to create games within the types of structures with which they are most familiar. Unfortunately for the children, who are the eventual recipients of adult games, this often means that competition against others is the guiding light. Therefore most adults (particularly males), as well as some heavily competitively conditioned children, may need to experience some cooperative-game alternatives before the creation process can flourish in a constructive direction.

It is interesting to note that over the past few years, when various groups of children have been given opportunities to create their own "fun" games, none of them has ever created games of hitting (such as football), games where large numbers of children remain inactive (such as baseball), or games where children are eliminated. These are adult concepts and not what children would create or choose on their own without conditioning by adults.

We have found that the younger the child, or the less conditioning a person has had to a highly competitive ethic, the more humane the game is likely to be. Even four- and five-year-olds can come up with some beautifully cooperative activities and demonstrate at the same time their wonderful imaginations. During a spring "potato party" a group of kindergarten children created the game of Mashed Potato. One was "potato" and the others were "milk" and were poured one at a time to stick to the potato. This was accomplished only with the child's imagination and a few "pouring" gestures. When they were all stuck in the group, they spontaneously jumped around still stuck, mashing everyone, to make a whole pot of mashed potatoes. The children invented the game completely on their own. A five-year-old girl was the ringleader, with ideas coming from several others. On another occasion a group of four-year-olds invented a hoop-dragging game, in which they took turns pulling each other around on their bellies with a hula hoop. All our experiences have demonstrated that children are never too young for constructive input. We just have to give them the chance.

In one attempt at creating new games I spoke to a group of 4th- and 5th-grade students and asked them to try to make up some new games or change old ones to make them more fun. I began by telling them what I was trying to do with my games: to have everyone participate and help one another, to let everyone have fun, and to have no one feeling like a loser. I gave a few examples of cooperative games that they had already played in the gym (Log Roll, Collective-Score Volleyball, Collective Stone) and told them they could use any equipment they wanted for their games. I asked them to split into groups of three or four, and away they went.

The creation process was beautiful to sit in on. Lots of creative ideas were flowing as the kids prepared to go down to the gym in about thirty minutes to try out some of their games. Children were working together, interacting verbally, sharing and refining ideas. When we went to the gym, each group had an opportunity to try out their game with their own little group in order to make any refinements necessary before teaching it to the class. For the next three gym classes the kids taught their games to their classmates. Following each game we

Putting our heads together

Agreeing on an idea

had a brief discussion session to get comments on the game and suggestions for improvement. The students were later given an opportunity to present and assess their refined game with another class. Two games were generally presented at the same time in different halves of the gym to keep the groups small.

Cooperative social interaction was apparent in the creation of the games, in the teaching of the games by the kids, in the playing of the games, in the evaluation of the games, and in the suggestions for improvement. I felt that the children came up with some very good games on very short notice. It was obvious from this game-creation process that the children understood the importance of participation and cooperation.

Marie Riley and Kate Barrett from the University of North Carolina in Greensboro are among the few who have involved themselves extensively in implementing what children have to offer in the way of game creation. Their child-designed games evolved primarily from classes of nine-, ten-, and eleven-year-olds who had previously been exposed to a games climate that allowed them to work at their own rate and to feel free to make mistakes. The overall games environment provided the opportunity for decision-making and choice between alternatives.

When I viewed some of these children playing their own games, I noted that there was no competition against others, no putting others down, no elimination of players, and rarely any set boundary lines. In the ball games there was lots of activity and a great deal of contact with the ball by *all* children. In one game (designed to include some element of striking), two children hit a ball back and forth over a net using many different body parts. The net was attached to the backs of two chairs. One of the children was highly skilled and could have easily drilled the ball past his partner, but he said, "Then there would be no game." Besides, he added, they were both "playing against the net."

What about games created by junior and senior high school students? I had the opportunity to speak to approximately 100 junior and senior high school students who were involved in conducting intramural programs in their own schools. This conference had been organized and was conducted by students for fellow students in the province who were interested in improving their intramural programs. Together we enjoyed an afternoon of Collective-Score Blanketball, Collective Monsterball Volleyball, Collective Orbit, Bump and Scoot, Cross-Over Dodgeball, and All-Touch Scooter Ball.

Afterward I asked the students to divide into small groups to discuss their feelings and to attempt to create some of their own alternatives. Many interesting comments and good suggestions for new or modified games were generated. One group wrote, "The more different or ridiculous a game is, the less competitive it is likely to be." For example, floor hockey played with a beach ball, basketball played with a monsterball, touch football played with a pumpkin, watermelon, or water balloon. Another group stated, "Teachers and students in collective sports would promote spirit and more people would feel inclined to try it. A better relationship between people would be developed."

Don Morris from Montana State University, one of the few who has looked to high school students for new designs in games, has also found teen-agers' input to be extremely valuable. When he asked a group of 9th-grade students to design a game that accounted for the different abilities of each student in the class, they came up with a modified version of softball in which seven bases were set up in a figure-8 pattern. Each batter could choose from a variety of different-sized balls and bats, as well as the manner in which the pitcher would deliver the ball. The more highly skilled players chose to use a regulation bat and softball thrown in the traditional manner, while some lesser-skilled students chose to have a large rubber ball rolled toward them and to strike it with an oversized, underweight bat. As in traditional softball, the batter had to hit the ball before leaving home plate and had to touch each base without being tagged out before returning home. However, each batter was allowed to stay at bat until the ball was hit forward and could then run to any base, at any time and in any order. Sometimes three people ended up on one base at one time.

In another game called Basketbowl players were given an opportunity to choose the manner in which they would contribute team points. They could opt to bowl the ball, throw it through a hula hoop, or shoot it into a basketball net.

Edward Devereux from Cornell University is a long-time proponent of child-directed games, even when (or especially when) the games being played were created neither by nor for children. His observations of children's pickup games led him to the following conclusions:

> When you watch a bunch of kids playing a self-organized game of sandlot baseball, it is clear that the emphasis is more on having fun than on winning. If the teams are out of balance, they see no problem in shifting one of the stronger players to the other team, right in the middle of the game. They pitch a bit more gently to the littler kids, so they can have some fun too; besides, since numbers are important, you really need them in the game. Errors are met with laughter and teasing more than with anger and derisive comment. As one kid remarked, "In our game, if everyone is tripping over everybody, it's just funny, but in the Little League the coaches get really mad because it's an important game." If the day is becoming too hot, or if the game has begun to lose interest, there's no problem in calling it quits and moving on to some other activity.

Working it out

All these experiences with youngsters have convinced me that we must depend more fully on the creative power of children and youth for alternatives. With a few simple guidelines they can often think in a way that has been conditioned out or made obscure by blinders in everyday adult life. They have the capacity to contribute so much more than we realize, toward their own learning and development and toward the betterment of our society. Why not give them the opportunity to do so?

Sample Games Created by Children and Youth

I have chosen fourteen games to share with you, eight of which were created by a group of nine- and ten-year-olds during one half-hour session and six of which were created by a group of teen-agers during another half-hour session.

CHILDREN'S GAMES

- *Action.* Each child chooses a partner, and they attempt to go through an action course together. The course consists of six stations, where partners: (1) bounce a large ball back and forth four times, (2) jump rope together ten times, (3) throw a small ball back and forth using a large scoop four times, (4) walk toward each other from opposite ends of a low balance beam, hold on to each other to turn around, and walk back, (5) bounce a ball back and forth four times, and (6) do a front roll on a mat, side by side. After completing this portion of the action course, the partners run directly back through the action line, jumping over the low beam and running between passing balls, and then turn around and run back straight through the action line and finish up by doing another roll and jumping into the air together.

    There were two lines side by side at the start of the course, much as in a normal relay. However, the children who were first in line worked together to complete the course, as partners. When the first pair went to the third station (scooping ball back and forth), the next pair started. It is interesting to note that on the return the kids came directly through the action rather than going around it to get back into line. The normal adult structure would have been to have the children return on the outside, away from where the other children were coming down the course.

- *Find Your Prey.* Each person gets a card with the name of a different animal on it, which is kept a secret. A list of animals is then read aloud that tells what prey each animal must find. The list is circular: for example, the elephant is looking for the lion, the lion for the wolf, the wolf for the dog, the dog for the cat, the cat for the mouse, and the mouse for the elephant. Without making any sound, each person then acts out the animal that is written on his or her card and attempts to find the animal acting like its prey. If a player thinks she's found her prey, she taps him on the head and the prey must show his card. If it's the right prey, the hunter holds on to him while he tries to find his prey. In the end there should be a single circle with all the animals holding on to each other.

    To add some additional challenge, the game creators made up decoy cards. One decoy card was distributed for every two or three animals. The decoys "can act like anything, to fool people." The decoys try to find one another and stay together.

    The four girls who made up this game could quickly adjust to accommodate different numbers of players by handing out a few additional animal cards, as long as the last animal was trying to find the first, so that the animals would eventually form a circle. This game was played in silence with no verbal cues; for younger groups, in addition to acting out the animal, they could make animal sounds.

- *Beat the Clock.* Two equal teams are formed on opposite sides of a volleyball net. A player on one team throws a volleyball over the net, and it is caught by a player on the other team and thrown back. If someone catches the ball for a second time, he must pass it to a person on his side who has not yet thrown it over the net. Once everyone on both teams has thrown the ball over the net, they check to see how long it took and then try to beat their record in the next game. A variation of this game is to have everyone on both sides catch the ball *and* pass to one of their own teammates to win the game. The children who invented this game felt that in order to make it really work they would have to come up with a way to "have more action"—a problem they had not yet solved when it was time to go.

- *Miss Your Legs.* The children break into groups of five, and the groups form lines 5 or 10 feet apart. The first person in each line hikes a ball under his legs to the next person and then runs to the back of the line. The second person then does the same thing, and so on down the line. One point is counted every time the ball is hiked to and successfully caught by the next person in line. After a specific time they can add up the collective score and then repeat the procedure to try to improve the first score.

- *In and Out.* This is a modified form of dodgeball. The group is divided into two, with one half forming a circle around the other half. The people on the outside of the circle throw a beach ball at those in the center. Two balls are in play. If the ball hits a player below the waist, he switches places with the person who threw it. This way everyone has a chance to be both inside and outside the circle, no one is really "out," and the beach ball "doesn't hurt."

  The students also suggested passing the ball once on the outside of the circle before throwing it to the center to increase cooperation. This suggestion was tried immediately and was well received. The game worked smoothly with a total group of about fifteen.

- *Cannon Defuser.* This game works best with four or five teams of about seven each. Each team has a ball and a tumbling mat in a different corner of the gym. One team member (cannon defuser) stands or kneels on the mat with a beach ball (cannonball) in his hands, while the other team members (paddlers) move their mat (ship) around the gym. The object is for the cannon defuser to direct his ship toward another ship and to shoot his cannonball at another cannonball. Once a throw is made, Paddler 1 retrieves the ball and becomes the cannon defuser, and the cannon defuser becomes a paddler. This continues until everyone has had a chance to be the cannon defuser. For a variation of this game, a cannon defuser remains a cannon defuser if he shoots and hits (defuses) a cannonball. This semicooperative game was very well received: lots of action, lots of laughter.

- *Gym Hattette.* Two teams are made up of six people each—the inventors chose three girls and three boys for each. Each team is trying to get six points. A point is scored when a baseball hat (puck) is directed into the opponents' goal with a stick or pole. Each team has a goalie, two defensive players, two forwards, and a center; the goals are the length of two gym mats (hanging on the wall); everyone on one team must touch the hat (by passing) before a team can score; a person can score only once during a game; the hat must be passed (not carried) over the center line.

This game was created by girls who presently play in a competitive ringette league within their community. Ringette is a relatively new girls' sport, which resembles noncontact floor hockey but is played with skates, on ice, with a ring

Explaining the rules

for a puck. The modified game (hattette) was well received once the rules became clear.

- *Baseball Tennis.* This game was created by kids playing in the streets of Ottawa. It is similar to regular street baseball in that you have a batter, a pitcher, and some fielders. However, a tennis racket is used as the bat and a bean bag is used as the ball. They first tried playing with a tennis ball, but "it went too far." So now they "chuck in" a bean bag. It works really well; there is no problem getting a "hit."

TEEN-AGERS' GAMES

- *Collective Blowball.* One person lies on his stomach on a mat while four to six others drag or carry the mat. The object is for the person on the mat to blow a ping-pong ball from a starting line to a finish line about 10 feet away. Once the ball goes over the finish line, the blower switches and becomes a carrier. The players can attempt to see how quickly they can have their whole team blow a ball back and forth between two lines, or how many times the ball can be blown back and forth in a certain time period.

For a variation, about five people lie on their stomachs in front of a starting line facing five others who are lying across a finish line. Several ping-pong balls are rolled out into the midpoint between the two lines. The collective objective is to blow the balls back and forth as many times as possible in a certain time span. The number of players and balls and the distance between lines are all very flexible.

- *Collective-Score Towel Ball.* This game is similar to Collective-Score Blanket-ball except that team members propel a beach ball over the net using towels. Players work in pairs within their teams. One collective point is scored every time the ball goes over the net and is caught by a pair on the other side. The ball must be passed to a second pair before being volleyed over. This game can also be played in groups of three or four and with towels of different sizes and shapes, chosen by players according to their ability and skill level. The number of pairs per side and the number of balls in play are also flexible.

- *Scooter Basketball.* In this game, similar to traditional cross-court basket-ball, each player sits on a little wooden scooter (similar to a small mover's dolly on casters) that allows free movement in any direction. The player propels himself by pushing off on the floor with his feet. Dribbling is optional. Every player on the team must touch the ball before attempting to score. Garbage cans

Playing the game

or European handball nets can be used as goals, two balls can be in play, and a collective scoring system can be applied.

- *Scooter Towel Ball.* This game is similar in structure to Scooter Basketball. Each player sits on a little wooden scooter but players work in pairs. Each pair has a towel, which they use together to catch, pass, and shoot. This game can be played using a traditional scoring procedure with a large goal, no goalie, and an "all-touch" rule (see page 70).

- *Partner Scooter Basketball.* This game is the same as Scooter Basketball except that one partner is on a scooter and the other is not. The standing partner pushes her mate around the court on the scooter but cannot touch the ball; the seated partner shoots at the goal or passes the ball to another player. Partners later switch positions. Different scoring options can be introduced to account for ability (e.g., shoot into a large net, through a hanging hula hoop, into a basketball net), and either traditional or collective scores can be counted.

CREATING YOUR OWN GAMES; EVALUATING YOUR SUCCESS

- *Basket-foot-ball.* This is a modified basketball game played with a football. There is generally no dribbling. The football is passed to every team member underhand before a shot is attempted. Two points are scored for the ball going through the hoop and one point for just hitting the backboard. The game begins with teams lining up facing each other, and one team hikes the ball. No body contact is allowed.

- *Other Teen-agers' Ideas.* For the Collective-Score Volleyball type of game, put blankets or sheets over the net so the receiving team cannot see exactly when the ball is coming over.

  In "all-touch" games, have some signal among team members (which is made up by team members) to indicate that you have not yet received the ball.

  Play ping-pong with five people around a big table to see how many times in a row you can get the ball over.

  Play flag football in deep snow.

  Play volleyball using the full length of the gym with all those who want to play playing at the same time.

Cooperative Play Days

At Cooperative Play Days a mixture of children from all grade levels (and adults too) can be integrated on a single team. They can teach one another the cooperative games they know and all play them together. They can create new cooperative games. It's a great way to bring children of various ages (or families) together, to allow them to get to know one another better, to teach others, to be concerned with one another, to be responsible for one another, and to help one another reach common ends. We have had many successful Cooperative Play Days both in and out of school settings. I would like to share with you one particularly unique Cooperative Games Day, which was spearheaded by Sally Olsen, a special-education teacher and mother of three. Sally has been a staunch supporter of co-op games over the past few years and was the inspiration behind the world's first bilingual, cooperative family play day. I asked her to recap the day in writing so that others could gain from her experience. What follows is her response to my request.

What a day! When we woke up the Ottawa fog was so thick you couldn't see the end of the driveway. When we arrived at Vincent Massey Park, it might as well have been raining, the dew was so heavy. But we set up, ever optimists, and at the appointed time people started coming and they kept coming. We spread out the parachute, which promptly got soaked on the grass, and the people congregated around it to start the Parachute game. We were cold and damp but soon the exercise and warm feelings of cooperating with others to have fun won out over the cold Ottawa day. We played most of the twelve games we had chosen and invented three more—all with a spirit of cooperation. What a day! We had a great time.

The organizing committee of three, with help from Terry, chose fourteen of the games in this book to play. These included:

Cooperative Musical Chairs	Bump and Scoot
Barnyard	Human Tangles
Toesies	Log Roll
Sticky Popcorn	Collective Orbit
Cooperative Musical Hugs	Blup-Blup-up-up
Parachute	Shoe Twister
Tiptoe Through the Tulips	Grasshopper

We chose the above list because we are a nursery school organization and we knew we would have a lot of preschoolers present. We chose all the games to use as little equipment as possible. Except for the two successful and unusual props—the parachute and a 10-foot weather balloon—we used some small beach balls and improvised the rest with the people present. When we didn't have chairs for Cooperative Musical Chairs, we used people with strong backs, who knelt, side by side, on all fours. We eliminated a chair when the music stopped, and the "chair" then got up to join the people skipping around and sitting. When we didn't have a net for Bump and Scoot, we got five people to join hands and be the net in the middle of the field. The "net" was allowed to hit the ball with their heads, knees or anything else they could manage without letting go of hands. They also moved from side to side on the field, which added some interest to the game.

In talking over the day, we thought the following ideas might be useful to anyone organizing a similar picnic:

Write the games out on a large Bristol Board. An example:

TOESIES

Maximum number in one group—an even number—10, 32. Kindergarten children giggle all the way through this game. Some older people have been known to let out a chuckle or two. Partners simply lie stretched out on the grass, feet to feet, and attempt to roll across the grass keeping their toes touching throughout. Variations: Try it with only the toes of the right feet connected, with legs crisscrossed. Try the whole thing with bare feet—we dare you!

We printed the games in French and English and drew a red border around the games that were most suited to preschoolers. We stapled the posters on sharpened 1″ x 2″ x 8′ poles with crosspieces made of lath. We suggest that you put out only four posters at the beginning of the day (for groups totaling 80 to 100). Musical Chairs, Human Tangles, Barnyard, and Parachute seemed to get people going. When people looked around for something new, we put up another poster. It was heartwarming to see games start up spontaneously throughout the day. Every once in a while a Sticky Popcorn group would erupt and spread over the field, gathering up everyone in their popping. The Log Rollers decided to finish their games by all rolling over the edge of a hill. We found that the parachute and the weather balloon were excellent in starting people off at the beginning of the day when the group was small and again after lunch when they tended to sit and ruminate too long.

You can buy a parachute from your local skydiving club. The weather balloons are found in surplus stores or in advertisements in magazines such as *Popular Science.* You don't need helium to blow up the balloons. Put the hose of your vacuum cleaner on the exhaust so that the hot air blows out and blows up the balloon. It is better to have several balloons, because they pop easily. We never blew ours up more than 5 feet in diameter.

We all agreed that it is better to have a supervisor at each game—someone who can get a group going but be able to let people take over and adapt or invent new games if they can. You also need an extra supervisor for games such as Co-op Musical Chairs if you are using people as chairs—someone to make sure no one sits on the chairs' heads or dives onto their backs. In Log Rolls we found that we needed someone to launch the rider in the proper manner and to help the riders off at the end so they wouldn't kneel on the last person. We also found that smaller children don't mix well with bigger ones for the logs. The smaller ones tend to slip down, and the rider might hit their heads with his knees.

We invented three games that day. The following version of Floating Parachute was passed on by a mother who played it in kindergarten with her child's class. You roll up the edge of the parachute (for a good grip) and pull gently until all the material touches the ground when laid flat. Try to get a large person pulling on each rib (the stitching forms the rib) and the smaller children pulling between the ribs. With everyone squatting down, get the parachute as flat on the ground as you can. A small child goes in the middle and lies down. Then everyone starts making waves in the parachute. Gradually make the waves bigger and bigger, and then someone with a loud voice yells, "One, two, three—up!" At this, everyone stands up and pulls the parachute waist-high. The child in the middle will float up about 2 feet. I'm sure they think it is much higher as the parachute billows in huge mountains of air around them. They will settle down fairly softly and they love it.

You may want to try it with an adult—someone said it would work but we didn't try it.

It seemed ironical to me that there were two Sunday school picnics in the park that same day and they were playing games like Tug of War and all the other competitive races that usually go along with picnics. I thought that their minister or pastor had probably just given them a sermon on brotherly love and helping one another and here they were trying their best to beat each other. Some were even provoked into cheating to win because they didn't have the physical skills to win fairly. How much better a day and a feeling they would have had if they had played cooperative games! Did we have a good day? Did we enjoy the games? As much as a traditional picnic? YES. We know you will too.

Evaluating Your Successes

If you want to know whether kids like a game or whether the game is fulfilling the desired objectives, you can carefully watch the children, listen closely to their not-so-idle chatter, and ask them some specific questions. Informal observations over an extended period of time provide some very valuable information. Questions to keep in mind include: Do the children understand how the game is supposed to be played? Is the challenge appropriate (too difficult, too easy, just right)? Is everyone involved in the action? Are the kids cooperating, helping, and sharing? Are they being considerate of others? Are the kids having fun? Do they look as if they feel accepted, or rejected? How do the children respond when you ask them if they want to play some games? Do they ask you to play the game(s)?

You can also get some important feedback during and after the games, in a variety of settings (in the gym, on the field, at the picnic, in the car, on the way to the locker room after a gym class, in the locker room, in the hall, at recess, in the classroom, in the home, and so on). Parents can often provide some very interesting comments from another perspective.

Should a negative response or "problem" arise within any of the above areas (e.g., a child left out, someone hogging the ball, someone hitting another, not enough action, etc.), try to assess where the structure has broken down, but also discuss the problem with the kids. See what they think should be done. Then immediately try to implement any of their positive suggestions so they know it's not just an exercise . . . you really do want their ideas! This same approach should be applied when you ask the children for constructive feedback right after they have played newly created games (mine, yours, or theirs). Give their ideas a try, the sooner the better.

When asking a group of children a question like, How did you like that game? I have found that the most aggressive or assertive kids—often boys—also tend to be most vocal in expressing their views. However, they often do not represent the feelings of the rest of the group, those not so outspoken in front of a group. It's important, therefore, to approach people individually, to seek out their personal feelings and suggestions. You can do this by talking to the players on a person-to-person basis, or, with a class perhaps, by having them fill out a brief questionnaire about the games they played. I've had a lot of success with this last method, maybe because having people ask children their opinions is a novel experience for them. For more ideas and a sample questionnaire, see the Appendix.

An important perspective that is often overlooked in many of our programs is firsthand experience by the leader, teacher, or assessor. If you want to know what's happening under the Big Turtle shell, what better way than to get under there? That way you not only hear what's going on but see it and feel it. You become part of the action! Besides, it's the best chance to learn something from the masters of playful play, the littlest children.

Beach-Ball Balance

where to go
from here

I hope that by now it's clear how strong our need is for alternatives in children's games and how exciting those alternatives can be. Somewhere we've gotten off the track, and I've tried in this book to suggest a few solutions to the problems that already exist, and to stimulate interest in going further and creating whole new systems of games. No one book can give you all the answers, but I hope that readers will go on in their own directions from the humble beginning we offer here. Be as flexible and imaginative as the games themselves.

We need to draw upon examples from other cultures and from our own past. We need to think more about creating contemporary "tying" games such as Taketak. We need to create more gentle games and more games of giving. Families and communities need to play together, with all members contributing toward a common end. Little children need to feel their own importance; older kids, to play with younger. When all kinds of people—young and old; big and small; male and female; black, white, and yellow—begin to work and play together, we will begin to make substantial progress toward a better environment for all.

If we put our brains to work and focus them on play, some functional thoughts about increasing sensitivity and restricting physical and psychological hurting will surely surface within the rules of contemporary games. Together we can then help those who follow us to inherit a healthier world in which to live and play.

postscript

When describing the various games in this book, in some cases I have purposely not outlined every single detail of precisely what to do and exactly when to do it. A certain amount of detail is necessary to get you going. But beyond that, detailed "rules" can make the games too rigid, when in fact they should be quite flexible. In addition, I have respect for my readers and feel certain you can come up with some things on your own, which leads me into the purpose of this postscript.

The games outlined in this book will probably be played by all kinds of people in a variety of settings: birthday parties, company picnics, gym classes, camps, preschools, classrooms, hospitals, therapy centers, detention homes, prisons, and so on. You will probably find that some of the games work extremely well for your purposes and others not so well. Once you start playing with cooperative games, I'm sure you will begin to adapt some of the games and to invent new ones that meet the needs of your particular situation. It would be a shame not to share your ideas and experiences so that others can benefit from them. So if you adapt or invent a new cooperative game or find that something you try works (or doesn't work), drop me a line. I'd love to hear about it and will make every effort to share the wealth of ideas that flow from your collective cooperative-games experience. This way we will all be winners. HAVE FUN!

Terry Orlick
School of Human Kinetics and
Leisure Studies
University of Ottawa
Ottawa, Ontario, Canada K1N 6N5

appendix a

Evaluation Methods

In order to get some detailed information and input from the various players, the following open-ended sample questions can be used either as a questionnaire or in an interview. Select or adapt those questions that seem suitable for your particular needs and age group. If you do not have time to ask all the questions, use the shortened form, the starred (★) questions.

When new rules are introduced (for example, "All Touch"):

    1. What did you think of those rules? Did you like them?

    2. How much fun was it to play using these new rules compared to regular rules?

   ★3. What was the best thing about the new rules?

★4. What was the worst thing about the new rules?

★5. What changes could we make in the new rules to make the game more fun?

6. Do you think you would want to play using these rules again? Once everyone was used to them?

When new *games* are introduced (for example, Log Roll):

1. What did you think of the game? Did you like it?
2. Who won? Did you win or lose?
3. Did you help in reaching the goal of the game? If yes, how?
★4. What did you like best about the game?
★5. What did you dislike most (or hate) about the game?
★6. Have you got any ideas on how to make it more fun? Or ways to make it better?
7. Would you like to play it again?

When a new games *program* is nearing completion (for example, after eight weeks of cooperative games):

★1. What did you think of the new games?
2. Did you like them?
3. What did you like best about the games?
4. What did you dislike most (or hate) about the games?
5. Did you usually feel happy or sad when playing the games?
★6. Which of the new games did you like best? Why?
★7. Which of the new games did you dislike most? Why?
8. Did you feel that you were helping one another in the new games?
9. Did you ever feel that you lost in the new games? If yes, (a) when and (b) how often? If no, why not?
10. Do you ever feel that you lose in regular games? If yes, (a) when and (b) how often? If no, why not?
★11. Do you have any ways to make new games better?
12. Do you have any ways to make regular games better?
13. If you could play any kinds of games you wanted in gym class (at a picnic, play days, etc.), what kinds of games would you play?
14. Would you have any special rules?

With the youngest game players, one simple means of finding out how you've succeeded is to use pictures, such as smiling and sad faces, to indicate feelings.

Immediately after the game is over, the players simply make a mark under the face with the expression closest to their feelings. With kindergarten children, we use three faces (happy, in-between, sad); with some retarded groups, just two faces (happy, sad); older groups respond to a range of five faces.

appendix b

Integrated Development Games

The following games were initially designed for a group of children, aged six to nine, who loved to move but had great difficulty sitting passively. These children had been assessed as having "learning problems" and were in a special-education class. The games were aimed at providing for active integrated development of social, academic, and physical spheres.

A major point to keep in mind when designing or using active games to develop intellectual, cognitive, or perceptual-motor skills is to tie in some cooperation component to allow for social-psychological development as well.

COOPERATIVE MATH AND SPELLING GAMES

- *Sum Games.* A pile of bean bags is placed at one end of the gym. The children stand in groups of four at the opposite end. The teacher calls out a number (e.g., "seven"), and each group of children runs to the bean bags and returns with the correct number. Each child must carry at least one bean bag. The children determine on their own how many bags each must pick up to solve the problem correctly. Once the children have the appropriate number of bags, they all run to the blackboard at the other end of the gym, step up on a bench to reach the board, and each chalk up the number of bags he or she has picked up. They then indicate the correct sign for addition and work together to add it up. The game incorporates the necessity for attentiveness to instructions, counting, addition, running, stepping up, and group interaction.

- *Target Toss.* Circular targets with two rings are placed at various points on the wall, one for every two children. The children work in pairs, one pitching and the other retrieving thrown balls. The pitcher takes five throws at the target. If she hits the wall or floor she gets one point; if she hits the large outside circle on the wall, she gets two points; and if she hits the smaller inside circle she gets three points. Each child keeps a mental record of her own score and after five shots runs to the blackboard and writes down her score. Once both partners have thrown, they work together to add up both of their scores, or the entire score for the group. They can then return to the target area and attempt to increase their collective score. This game incorporates throwing skills, retrieval of balls for partner, short-term retention of numbers, addition, and the concept of collective score.

- *Pot of Gold.* A pot (cardboard box) containing bags of gold (bean bags) is placed at one end of the gym. The children know how many bags of gold are in their pot, which they share together in their small group. The children then decide on an object that they would like to "buy" (e.g., a shovel) and the miner (teacher) tells them the cost (i.e., number of bean bags). Together the groups then run to the pot and pull out the gold necessary. Each child must carry at least one piece. Through subtraction they must then find out how much gold is remaining in the pot. When they think they know how much gold is remaining, they run to the other end of the gym to tell the miner. When they are correct, they return the gold to their pot and begin a new game by selecting another item to buy. The game incorporates the concepts of subtraction and sharing in a running game.

- *Spelling Ball.* The children divide into pairs, each pair sharing a ball. The pairs then attempt to go through the letters in the alphabet as they pass the ball back and forth. As a child passes the ball to his partner, he calls out the next letter. The same procedure can be followed to spell each other's names, animal names, colors, and so on. If one child is unsure of the next letter, his partner can give him a hint by drawing the shape of the letter in the air. The type of ball and kinds of passes used can be varied.

In a more advanced version of this game for older children, two teams, one on either side of a net, play a volleyball-type spelling game with a balloon or beach ball. The two teams first decide on a word to spell. When the ball goes over the net, the whole team on the side that hit the ball over quickly forms the first letter with their bodies. When the ball is batted back over, the whole team on the other side forms the second letter, and so on until the whole word is completed. The teams can either catch or volley the ball.

Spelling games can also be played underwater. A team decides on a word, and each individual becomes responsible for a specific letter. The players then dive to the bottom of the pool and write their letter on an underwater writing board. In games such as this, words can be introduced that represent themes of cooperation and friendship.

- *What's the Action?* Small groups of children watch as a teacher demonstrates an action (jump, skip, etc.). The children then think of a word that fits the action, locate the letters required to spell the word from a group of alphabet cards spread out on the floor, put the letters in the proper order, and write the word on the blackboard with each child in the group being responsible for one letter. The whole group then moves around the room together, doing what the word says.

- *Spell Sport.* Children divide into teams of about four to nine. Two sets of alphabet cards are provided for each team. The teams line up at the near end of the room; the lettered cards, including a period and exclamation mark, are scattered at the far end of the room. The teacher calls out the name of a sport, or gives clues about the word to be spelled (e.g., played on a mat, two people involved, contact sport, nine-letter word). Each team then has a minute to work out their strategy before running to their set of letters. Each player must pick up a letter and return to the starting line. The whole team then spells the given word by lining up in proper order.

This game elicits cooperation among team members but not between different teams, if more than one team exists. To ensure cooperation among *all* participants, the various teams can work together to spell a word sequence or sentence. Words can be adapted to the age level and size of group. Certain players may have to pick up more than one letter, but every player must always have at least one letter.

Here's a variation for younger children: Place a series of numbered cards at the end of the room. Each child runs down to pick up one number. The children then arrange themselves in numerical order, ascending or descending.

COOPERATIVE PERCEPTUAL
MOTOR DEVELOPMENT GAMES

The following games illustrate how cooperative social interaction and perceptual-motor development can be integrated into the same activity.

• *Co-op Paint-In.* This activity improves children's eye-hand coordination and vertical jumping abilities in a situation involving group cooperation. The children are divided into groups of four, preferably of varying heights. Outlines of various geometric shapes are drawn on paper and taped to a wall at a level slightly higher than the children's arm's reach, making it necessary for the children to jump in order to mark the drawing. The children are asked to dip their index fingers into a pot of thick paint, select a point on the outline of the drawing, jump up, and mark this point with their painted finger. By taking turns jumping and marking, the team eventually covers the entire outline of the shape. Each group works cooperatively as the children who can jump higher become responsible for marking the higher limits of the drawing, and the children who cannot jump as high fill in the sides and the base line of the figure. This paint-in approach can be modified to introduce the fundamental concepts of printing (e.g., making the circles and lines which will eventually form letters).

• *Matilda.* This game was designed to increase the children's awareness of body parts and to develop the concept of right-side and left-side orientation as it pertains to another person's body. The teacher acts as puppeteer, and a child or assistant acts as Matilda, the puppet. The children are told that Matilda is getting ready to go outside and needs all their help to dress warmly and properly. The puppeteer discusses the articles of clothing that Matilda will need to keep warm and reviews the different body parts to be clothed. Other articles that Matilda needs to function in her daily routine are also mentioned. As the teacher points out these articles, a child is asked to come up and place the object on

Matilda. The puppeteer might say, "Here are Matilda's keys. She needs them to lock the door. She places them in the right back pocket of her pants." A child will then be asked to place the keys in Matilda's right back pocket. Matilda may also "need warm socks to wear before she goes out to play, one on her right foot and one on her left foot." For right and left articles of clothing, such as socks, gloves, and shoes, two children can come forward and dress Matilda together, identifying which arm, leg, hand, or foot they are dressing. Once Matilda is all dressed and has her watch, ring, wallet, bus ticket, and so on in the proper place, the puppeteer reviews with the children each article and where it has been placed.

This puppet-puppeteer approach greatly increases the fun component and helping component of learning about laterality and body parts. With larger groups, more than one puppet can be used. To increase the active component, children can run from one end of the gym to the other end to dress Matilda. It is also possible for all the children to dress the puppet or puppets at the same time, each being responsible for a different item.

COOPERATIVE DYNAMIC BALANCE ACTIVITIES

These activities have been introduced to develop an awareness of the effect and direction of gravity, and to have the children work together to gain some perception of their bodies in relation to themselves, other people, and their environment. It is particularly important in some of the games to make sure players are carefully "spotted," (followed and watched) by other players and supervisors, in case of falls. Some examples of these activities are outlined below.

Balancing Progression from Floor to Balance Beam

1. *Tray Balance on Floor*
Each pair of children is given a board or tray with a block on it. Each child holds one end of the tray, and together they walk across the gym floor, one walking forward and the other backward. The children attempt to reverse directions without bumping into the wall.

2. *Tray Balance on Beam*
The two children repeat the above procedure on a wide board or on a balance beam, depending upon their capabilities. The children are encouraged to warn

their partners when they are approaching the end of the beam or preparing to change direction.

3. *Wand Balance on Beam*
The children are given two long sticks or wands, which they hold as if they were holding a stretcher. A third wand is placed across the other two wands. The children attempt to walk across the beam without letting the third wand fall off. A ball can also be placed on the two wands.

4. *Object Balance Between Body on Beam*
Two children put a pillow between their heads or a wand between their bodies. Then, without touching the object with their hands, they attempt to walk across the beam. The object is held by the mutually applied pressure. To be done successfully, this game involves close continuous awareness of the other person. If the partners do not move in a synchronized manner, either the object will fall or one child will nudge the other off balance.

• *Joy's Inclination.* Two parallel benches are propped up securely against a jungle gym or stall bars so that they are slightly inclined. The children are first asked to walk forward and then backward on the sloping bench, with their partner spotting them. Two children then hold hands and walk side by side on the two sloping benches, first forward and then backward. They then turn and face each other and side-step up and down the benches, holding hands. The side step is repeated with the children balancing a ball between two sticks while traveling up and down the benches.

For a more advanced game, the children can toss a ball back and forth as they climb up and down the benches. Two children can also face each other, hold hands, and walk up and down on one sloping bench with one going forward and the other going backward. As a final progression, two children can begin by standing at opposite ends of the same sloping bench, walk toward each other, and meet at the center of the bench. The children then try to develop a cooperative method to pass each other, so that each child can continue up or down the bench to the other end. We try to encourage verbal communication and also encourage children to come up with imaginative stories as to why they have to cross the bridge without stepping off.

• *Teeter-Totter Crosswalk.* Two benches are set up at right angles to each other with one bench balancing on top of the other in a teeter-totter fashion. (Benches constructed with a crossbar at the base should not be used, as they tend not to balance properly.) Each child walks from one end of the top bench to the other, beginning with one end of the bench touching the floor and ending up with the other end touching the floor (like a teeter-totter). Two spotters can hold the balancing child's hands as he walks across the bench.

As a variation two children can attempt to position themselves on either end of the top bench (teeter-totter) in order to make it balance. A more difficult version for seasoned balancers begins with one child standing or kneeling on each end of the top bench. While keeping the bench balanced, each child attempts to move across the bench to the other end. Since there are two children balancing on the same bench, they must cooperate and devise a way to move across the teetering bench and pass each other on the bench in order to reach the other end. Holding hands with a partner on the floor, or some form of spotting, may be necessary initially.

appendix c

Fun in Intramurals*

IMPLEMENTATION OF HOPKINS ALTERNATIVE

1. Inform people of the nature of the program, pointing out that there are no awards or officials and that low skill level is totally acceptable.

2. Promote the fun and other positive social aspects of the program.

3. Adjust the rules to maximize play, to ensure equality and safety, to minimize injury, and to reduce the emphasis on skill.

4. Make it easier to enter the program, with no eligibility rules or formal structure. Simply allow groups of friends to enter and emphasize that individuals can be accommodated through the intramural coordinator.

---

* The material in this Appendix was provided by Peter Hopkins, Director of Intramurals, University of Waterloo, Waterloo, Ontario.

5. Encourage teams to make up distinctive, humorous names.

6. Hold an organizational meeting for all captains, and at the meeting:

a. Re-emphasize the philosophy of the program.

b. Inform the captains that they are responsible for the good order and conduct of the game.

c. Make it clear that undesirable conduct will be dealt with in an appropriate manner—expulsion from the league.†

d. Ensure that they know that there is a means to provide input and to air their grievances.

e. Ask the captains to phone the coordinator the day after their game to discuss the game (not the score), the rules, and whether they had fun.

f. Ask the captains to discuss the rules before each game, and if problems arise during the game, to stop the game and hold a meeting.

g. Inform everyone of the equal-number concept. If both captains agree to play with seven in volleyball, play with seven.

h. Inform everyone that if one team does not have enough players, the other team should share.

i. If a team can't make a game, have the captain call a replacement team to play instead.

j. Ask the participants what rules they want to adopt.

k. Inform the participants about the safety aspects of the program.

l. Ask the participants how they wish to conclude the league—e.g., an extra game, a challenge night, a fun play day, a tournament (if a tournament is chosen, ensure that it is open for all teams to enter and that everyone plays a minimum of two games).

7. Re-emphasize the nature of the program.

8. On the schedule, put positive statements like "The important thing in athletic sports is not the winning but the taking part."—Pierre de Courbetin.

9. Call the leagues the Birds and the Bees, the Co's and the Ed's, rather than A, B, C, or 1, 2, 3.

10. Go out and observe the program and talk with the participants to get their point of view.

11. When writing an article about the program, talk about the people and the humorous things that happened, not about the score and standings.

---

† The author of this book suggests that if an alternative fun league is set up and a player in this league has a complaint against him/her he/she be informed of the complaint, and upon receiving a second complaint that he/she be transferred to the competitive league. After a certain time he/she may return to the fun league on a trial basis.

12. Evaluate the program not simply with numbers but by sending out an open opinionaire to all participants, asking their point of view.

13. Allow for adequate and appropriate facility time, and budget for an expanded program in the future.

14. Adapt the participants' ideas into the next program.

15. Watch the participants having fun.

SUGGESTED ACTIVITIES

The following team activities have been implemented into the Hopkins Alternative for men, women, and mixed teams.

1. *Indoor Soccer:* No offsides; floating goaltender; walls in play; no body contact; keep ball below the shoulders; unlimited players on each team; equal numbers.

2. *Volleyball:* Equal numbers; play until time expires; if mixed, suggest that both sexes should hit the ball before it goes over, if hit more than once; could try unlimited hits on each side.

3. *Touch Football:* One-handed touch; defensive team makes the call "touch"; ball is dead if it hits the ground; no blocking; unlimited forward passing; everyone is an eligible receiver.

4. *Ball Hockey:* Suggested number depends on facility or desire of teams; no offsides; walls in play; keep sticks below waist, no one allowed in creases; no bodychecking in walls; no cross-checking; free substitution; cannot score from own half of floor.

5. *Basketball:* Suggest three on three for men's or women's but six for mixed basketball; mixed basketball rules: no men can handle the basketball in either key—that is, no passing, checking, rebounding, driving, or shooting in the key; free substitution; no jump balls, only possession and start play over; scoring: men—2 points; women—4 points in, 3 points if ball hits rim, 2 points if ball hits backboard.

6. *Slow-Pitch Softball:* Pitch to your own team; pitch until batter hits; ten to twelve per side (equal numbers); unlimited substitution; each inning, total side hits once around the order; side out when the ball from last batter gets to home plate; if mixed, two women should play in the infield.

7. *Hockey:* Equal numbers; unlimited substitution; no slap shots; no bodychecking; some play no goalie; no face-offs—just possession; no offsides, or center line only for offsides; suggest no raising puck (or sponge puck); minimal equipment needed—helmets, shin guards, and athletic support (last item men only); if goalies are used, they use full equipment; after a goal, other team's possession and rush.

8. *Broomball:* Equal numbers; unlimited substitution; no offsides; goalies cannot pass ball over the center line; roof, walls, are in play; after a goal, other team's rush; no bodychecking; no high brooms (not over waist); helmets necessary; turnovers for possession; if mixed, suggest three men out, three women out, and one of either in goal; if broomball shoes are permitted, have a league with shoes and a league without shoes, for equal play.

9. *Water Polo:* Put everyone in inner tubes, except the goalie; men may catch or throw with one hand, women with two; goalies cannot pass ball past center line; no rings or other jewelry; free substitution; equal numbers; can play the ball only when in tube; no excessive dunking; suggest that everyone wear shirts.

recommended reading

If you want some additional cooperative games or games nobody loses, I suggest you read the following booklets:

For the Fun of It: Selected Cooperative Games for Children and Adults (1975), by Marta Harrison and the Non Violence and Children Program. For copies write to Non Violence and Children, Friends Peace Committee, 1515 Cherry Street, Philadelphia, Pennsylvania 19102.

All Together: A Manual of Cooperative Games (1950), by Theo F. Lentz and Ruth Cornelius. Write to Peace Research Laboratory, 6251 San Bonita, St. Louis, Missouri 63105.

Cooperative Games: For Indoors and Out (1974), by Jim Deacove. Write to Family Pastimes, RR #4, Perth, Ontario, Canada K7H 3C6.

Learning Through Noncompetitive Activities and Play (1977), by Bill and Dolores Michaelis. Write to Learning Handbooks, 530 University Avenue, Palo Alto, California 94301.

For a collection of additional "new games," some of which are beautifully cooperative, some of which are not, I refer you to:

The New Games Book (1976), edited by Andrew Fluegelman. Write to the New Games Foundation, P.O. Box 7901, San Francisco, California 94120.

If you have a child who participates in any organized sport (such as baseball, soccer, football, hockey, swimming, etc.), for his or her sake I urge you to read:

Every Kid Can Win (1975), by Terry Orlick and Cal Botterill. Write to Nelson Hall Publishers, 325 West Jackson Boulevard, Chicago, Illinois 60606.

If you really want to understand the depth of the competition problem in our society and the many means toward positive solutions (for the sake of your own sanity and the sanity of our culture), read *Winning Through Cooperation: Competitive Insanity, Cooperative Alternatives*. It provides a very thorough look at cooperative structures (including games), cooperative cultures, cooperative values, and many constructive means for improving the quality of our lives.

Winning Through Cooperation: Competitive Insanity: Cooperative Alternatives (1977), by Terry Orlick. Write to Hawkins & Associates Publishers, 729 Delaware Avenue, S.W., Washington, D.C. 20024.

OTHER INTERESTING RELATED WORKS

Cratty, B. J. *Learning About Human Behavior Through Active Games.* Englewood Cliffs, N.J.: Prentice Hall, 1975.

Dauer, V. P., and Pangrazi, R. P. *Dynamic Physical Education for Elementary School Children.* Minneapolis: Burgess Publishing Company, 1975.

Evans, D. *Oh Chute: Parachute Activities for Fun and Fitness* (1971). Write Fun and Fitness, 701 East 38th Street, Sioux Falls, South Dakota 57105.

"Games Teaching." *Journal of Physical Education and Recreation.* Special feature on games for elementary school children, September 1977.

Mauldon, E., and Redfern, H. B. *Games Teaching: A New Approach for the Primary School.* London: Macdonald and Evans, 1969.

Morris, G. S. *How to Change the Games Children Play.* Minneapolis: Burgess Publishing Company, 1976.

Orlick, E., and Mosley, J. *Teacher's Illustrated Handbook of Stunts*. Englewood Cliffs, N.J.: Prentice Hall, 1963.

Schneider, T. *Everybody's a Winner: A Kids' Guide to New Sports and Fitness*. Boston: Little Brown and Co., 1976.

Smoll, F., and Smith, R. (eds.). *Psychological Perspectives in Youth Sports*. Washington, D.C.: Hemisphere Publishers, 1978. See in particular chapter on co-operative-game evaluation.

Recommended record to use when young children are playing cooperative games:

"Singable Songs for the Very Young" (1976), Sung by Raff; Troubadour Records (TR-002-C 1), Box 371, Station 2, Toronto, Ontario, M5N 2Z5.

index

About the Author

Terry Orlick is professor and researcher in the psychology of sport and physical activity at the University of Ottawa. A graduate of Syracuse University, the College of William & Mary, and the University of Alberta, he is also a former Eastern intercollegiate and NCAA regional gymnastics champion. In recent years, he has been very active in developing and promoting cooperative game programs in schools and daycare centers throughout the world. His other works include *Every Kid Can Win; Winning Through Cooperation: Competitive Insanity, Cooperative Alternatives; In Pursuit of Excellence;* and *The Second Cooperative Sports & Games Book.*